THE SHOp

D1355010

About the Editors

Hilary Wakeman was co-editor with John Wakeman of THE SHOp from 2001 to its closing in 2014. She has been a librarian, journalist, small-time farmer and mother of five. Hilary was one of the first women priests in the Church of England, and subsequently one of the first women rectors in the Church of Ireland. She is the author of *Saving Christianity: New Thinking for Old Beliefs* and three other titles.

Hilary Elfick is the author of numerous collections of poetry and a novel. Her Polynesian interpretation of Shakespeare's *The Tempest* brought considerable interest from the international Shakespeare community. She has performed her work in cathedrals, theatres, bookshops, libraries, schools and at literary festivals in many countries around the world.

BAINTE DEN STOC

WITHDRAWN FROM
DÚN LAOGHAIRE-RATHDOWN COUNTY
LIBRARY STOCK

BAINTE DEN STOC

WITHDRAWN FROM
DÚN LAOGHAIRE-RATHDOWN COUNTY
LIBRARY STOCK

THE SHOp

AN ANTHOLOGY OF POETRY

BAINTE DEN STOC

WITHDRAWN FROM
DÚN LAOGHAIRE-RATHDOWN COUNTY
LIBRARY STOCK

Edited by
Hilary Wakeman and Hilary Elfick

BAINTE DEN STOC

WITHDRAWN FROM
DÚN LAOGHAIRE-RATHDOWN COUNTY
LIBRARY STOCK

The Liffey Press

Published by

The Liffey Press Ltd

'Clareville'

307 Clontarf Road

Dublin D03 PO46, Ireland

www.theliffeypress.com

© 2020 By the individual authors and illustrators

A catalogue record of this book is
available from the British Library.

ISBN 978-1-9160998-9-0

All rights reserved. No part of this publication may be reproduced or transmitted in
any form or by any means, including photocopying and recording, without written
permission of the publisher. Such written permission must also be obtained before
any part of this publication is stored in a retrieval system of any nature. Requests for
permission should be directed to The Liffey Press, 'Clareville',
307 Clontarf Road, Dublin D03 PO46, Ireland.

Printed in Spain by GraphyCems.

CONTENTS

FAMILIES

BIRTH

GROWING UP

LOVE, ONE TO ONE

LIVES

OLD AGE

DYING

DEATH

FUNERALS

LOSS AND BEREAVEMENT

NATURE

IN OTHER PLACES

RELIGION

List of Illustrators

Nick Bridson Baker, p. 14

Beverley Gene Coraldean, p. 70

Luis Fanti, pp. 62, 254, 275

Valerie Gleeson, p. 57

Denise Hogan, p. 40

Alice Hoult, p. 134

Hammond Journeaux, pp. 22, 98, 140, 155, 167

Brian Lalor, pp. 11, 213

Peter Mabey, p. 179

Jeanette McCulloch, pp. 45, 55, 129, 137, 149, 230, 266, 277

John Minihan, p. 119

Mary Norman, p. 104

Peadar O'Donoghue, p. 164

Joakim Säflund, p. 37

Edwin Smith, p. 281

Matthew Wakeman, p. 60

Theo Wakeman, p. 52

Acknowledgements

The first people to thank are the 960 poets whose work appeared in THE SHOp in the fifteen years in which it was published because they were the reason for its existence. Thanks also to the many people whose artwork was requested to fit specific poems. And of course to the poets and artists who have so freely given permission to re-publish their work in this anthology. We have tried to contact all 285 selected poets and the 17 artists and photographers, but inevitably, six years after THE SHOp closed its doors, some have been untraceable.

In order to make this book as similar as possible to the original magazines, whose physical presence was so much appreciated, unusually high production costs were incurred. An Arts Council Award might have solved the problem but the timing just would not have worked. Instead, we relied on the enthusiasm and generosity of a large number of SHOp fans. We are so very grateful to each one of them. As we are to all those who were Sponsors and Friends of The SHOp over the years. With heartfelt thanks we remember Seamus Heaney, whom we were awed to have from the beginning as our Patron, anonymous (by choice) until now.

This anthology would not be here if it were not for one former subscriber, Alec, long-term friend of John Wakeman, the founder and editor of THE SHOp. Alec emailed me on April 3rd this year, asking, 'Why isn't there a SHOp anthology?' Within 24 hours his question had caught on. Theo Dorgan was supportive, and so were a couple of poets with whom I happened to be in correspondence at the time. On April 4th, my friend Hilary Elfick said she wanted to be involved at which point we knew it had to happen. On April 5th Alec emailed again: 'That was a daffy idea. Forget it.' Too late, Alec.

We want especially to thank Theo Dorgan for writing the Foreword, for his keenness that the book should come into existence and his help and advice at every stage. Thanks also to Gabriel Rosenstock who, as in earlier years, made sure that poems in Irish were as they should be. And thanks to Brian Lalor for the cover image: its first SHOp appearance was on the cover of issue 43.

My co-editor Hilary Elfick and I want to thank David Givens of The Liffey Press, whose immediate response to our proposal was, 'I'd be delighted.' And I personally want to thank Hilary for her patience and her persistence in getting everything right. The three of us have had a really good experience of working together as a team, an experience which will not soon be forgotten.

Hilary Wakeman
Norwich
October 2020

In April 2000 the poet Joan Poulson gave me, for my birthday, a year's subscription to a new poetry magazine. I'm now among the contributors who possess a copy of every edition of THE SHOp, without which I could not have worked with the other Hilary through a pandemic. She was in Norwich, I'm in Cambridge, and we only met once this year – a carefully guarded few sunny hours by the sea in North Norfolk.

We are similar in age, vision and doggedness, were already friends, now colleagues. Neither of us owns state-of-the-art apparatus, and our operating systems did not match. Most records no longer existed either on disk or hard drive. Immediate decisions were: to include as many poets as possible, to reflect the range of subject matter and style in the original issues, and to be honest when we doubted each other's choices.

So many on-line discussions – What makes a poem? Is just liking a poem enough? Does a big name outrank a new solitary voice? The anthology does not reflect the numbers of times a poet was published by John and Hilary, and some important poets' work was rejected, however reluctantly. Other poets' first publication was in an issue of THE SHOp. Of those, some returned, some disappeared, yet their poem which first caught the Wakemans' attention still catches ours.

Poets are jostling to write about the pandemic. For us two, this time will be most remembered for the creation of this anthology. And for the way David Givens of The Liffey Press became, seamlessly, the other part of a triangle. But our backcloth was always the widespread murmurs of excitement and encouragement from the poets and artists who found a home in this extraordinary magazine.

Hilary Elfick
Cambridge
October 2020

FOREWORD

It takes, some might say, a certain high-minded madness to found a poetry magazine – not just to take on editing, designing and paying for the thing, but to voluntarily open your postbox to those many thousands convinced, for better or worse, that what the world most urgently needs is the opportunity to read their poems. If there is a sober angel of sanity who helps to top and override that kind of madness, John and Hilary Wakeman must surely have had its beneficence hovering over them when they established THE SHOp.

Consider the circumstances: John had been co-founder of, and had for twelve years edited, that excellent English poetry journal, *The Rialto*. A poet himself, he had edited numerous reference books on world literature and on world film directors for the H.W. Wilson Co. of New York. When they moved to West Cork – Hilary had been appointed one of the first women rectors of the Church of Ireland – one might be forgiven for thinking that a combination of semi-retirement and new responsibilities might have tempted them to relax into the lotus land of the hills around Schull, easing themselves into a deserved peace by the paradoxically placid waters of Roaringwater Bay. Instead, John decided to found what would become, though he could not have expected it, a beloved and much-admired poetry magazine that made an immense contribution to poetry in Ireland and the wider world. When Hilary retired in 2001 she became co-editor and took over as designer from Joachim Säflund. You will bear in mind, please, that John was seventy years of age when he embarked on this – Hilary, as we all know, enjoys the grace of being forever young.

THE SHOp was a resounding success from the very start. As John told Arminta Wallace, in a 2012 interview in *The Irish Times*, 'I was amazed by the people who gave me poems for a magazine that didn't even exist.' That first issue, by invitation only, featured among its contributors Medbh McGuckian, Derek Mahon, Brendan Kennelly and John Montague. It says something about the editor's personality that he could attract such luminaries, but in the fifteen years of the magazine's life the trust of those early contributors would be more than justified. To be invited to submit to THE SHOp, or to offer a contribution and have it accepted, became a badge of honour, a source of delight. At its peak, the magazine might publish 150 poems from 6,000 or so submitted – John and Hilary read every one of those 6,000, replying to submissions with a promptness and friendly informality that surprised and pleased us all.

What was it about THE SHOp that had President Higgins write: 'Over the period between 1999 and 2014, the SHOp was recognised as one of the most beautiful poetry journals of the period'? What was it that had Bernard O'Donoghue describe it as 'unquestionably the most beautiful poetry magazine now in existence', or prompted that upright man Seamus Heaney to confess to being 'a confirmed SHOp-lifter'? Graciousness is part of the explanation – the magazine was always spaciously laid out, giving room for the poems to breathe, and the spare but telling illustrations, from artists such as John Minihan and Basil Blackshaw, added immensely to the sheer physical pleasure of holding this publication in your hands. For me, there was another level of beauty to be savoured though; let's call it the confirmation of constant happy surprise. THE SHOp was always hospitable to new voices, as well as to new work from familiar ones, so that in every issue you could count on finding poems that had you reaching for the phone or the keyboard to spread the word about something good and fine that had caught your eye. In this way, THE SHOp didn't just publish poems, drawings and photographs; it helped build and affirm a sense that these things matter – a crucial contribution to civility during the crass and overbearing years of the ill-fated boom.

To our widespread grief, John died in 2018. Now Hilary, still going strong, with her co-editor Hilary Elfick, has done us the great service of compiling an anthology representative of those 15 wonderful years, bringing back to readers and contributors alike the happiest memories of a magical magazine and of her beloved John, a gift to light up our lives again in this new kind of darkness. William Wall had it right when he wrote that, 'The success of the magazine was in large part due to the SHOpkeepers themselves.' For what they gave us, for their service and dedication, for their belief that poetry really does matter, we have cause to be truly grateful.

Theo Dorgan
Dublin
October 2020

HOME

Frank Redpath   *Miss White*

Chaps of my age, who've learnt it's better to
Stay fast asleep, half-wake at night and go
Fumbling along the landing to the loo;
Don't switch the light on, sit to have a pee,
Lean on the opened door edge: so,
Try to preserve insensibility.

It never worked: the thin white cat would hear,
Who slept, long-legged and awkward on the stair.

Aloof by day, a stalking elegance
Who rarely purred, but sometimes would bestow
Favour upon my knee and butt my chin,
What I'll miss now is that surprising ghost
Who'd march in there to join me, climb into
My dropped pyjama trousers, make a nest.

Absurd familiar I named Miss White,
Gone, now, taking your gift: laughter at night.

Michael Davitt   *An Sioc*

Cad eile 'bheadh uaim sa tsaol:
cead teachta is imeachta
gan aird ar éinne

is an oíche ag titim le faobhar
is an sioc ag tuirlingt ón spéir
is an fuacht ag crapadh na réalt?

Cad eile 'bheadh uaim sa tsaol:
bheith neadaithe isteach
fé charn blancéadaí

is an sioc amuigh ina shuí
is an fuacht ag siúl timpeall an tí?
Cad eile 'bheadh uaim sa tsaol:

muga breá tae le héirí gréine
is canta aráin agus im air
agus subh bhreá mhilis shú craobh

is an dúthaigh chomh bán le heala
is an lá chomh cruaidh le speal
is an intinn chomh geal is chomh géar?

Michael Davitt   *The Frost*

What more could I want in life:/to come and go/whenever I choose

as the edgy night comes down/ and frost spreads over the ground/
and the stars are shrunk by the cold.

What more could I want in life/to nestle in/under a pile of blankets/

as the frost sits down outside/ and the cold walks over the floor./
What more could I want in life:

a mug of strong tea at break of day/ and a thick cut of buttered toast/
sweetened with raspberry jam

and the country is white as a swan/and the day as hard as a scythe/
and the mind is as sharp and as bright.

Prose translation by Michael Davitt

Daniel Hardisty   *Distances*

Now try to imagine your journey home:
no matter the place you started from, or what
little you have packed for the distance;
the map mislaid, the app on your mobile
short of battery, setting off as simply
as the boat slips from the shore and drifts.
Where are you heading; what houses are those?
Does the city dilute into the suburbs,
or do the rows of childhood's terraces
rise in tides to meet you: where your clothes
hang in tender greys across the street
and the football slaps against the middens
(where a white stave of wickets are painted
by hand between two battered goal posts)
and voices call to you in your own voice
from old doorsteps, their names forgotten.
Or can you no longer pinpoint the place?
Only this rented room, your suits creaking
in the wardrobe; the man pacing upstairs;
the night-time sounds as the boiler rattles
to life and the moon studies the curtain.
Close your eyes, listen for the voice
that drifts across the corporation grounds:
we carried on our games, there is space for you,
now tell us why no-one has called us home.

Frank Golden   *This Time*

My father would come this time of year
The hawthorn needled into flower
The sycamore and elder in full leaf
To relish a call that ravelled him back in time.

It takes whole seasons to map a valley
To find a mushroom stone on a high bluff
To deepen the veined trace of rising tracks
To source the mill race on a vanished river.

It takes time for the weave of rustlings and calls
To engrain or simply settle, and for the body
To move as a common element,
To fold in with the daily course of light and rain.

Our instinct for home
Our desire for the physic hill
Or the ample body, or the absolute sky,
Or the dawn song on the still crest,

The ordained moment
Like finding the cuckoo's call nesting in your hand,
Or in the furlong field watching
The braiding course of a daylight fox.

It was always the cuckoo that he came to hear,
Like a tailwind ride downhill
Or seagulls in the wake of home bound boats,
There was a freedom in it, a tuning

To a world of constants, grassheads rising,
The long lane full of uncurling fern,
Faith that the fact of their occurrence,
Made plain the numinous chorus to our lives.

Jenny Joseph   *Makers*

Of my chair

Three wicker wands
Made with hands
That think nothing, but know
That this is how they're meant to go.
Not for any reason
Except that it is so.
It is the chair he's good at making, not the thought.

Of my candlestick

Here was a calm man
Knew how to put three curves together.
If I could bend a piece of metal so
As to coil the arc my fingers bent, round hearts
There would be nothing in words I'd need to do or know.

Paul Muldoon   *The Outhouse*

This would have been a night in late August,
somewhere in or around the turn of the century, when a little gust
bestirred itself from Lake Champlain
and he himself got up, as a dead man might get up, from where he'd lain

to find his way over that ever-treacherous rise
in the yard. Some version of the outhouse still stood and – surprise, surprise –
as he unbuttoned himself to answer this "call of nature"
he found himself staring straight at his own majuscule signature.

What with the slightly unhinged seat, the spiked news-stories, the dead dog scent
of lilac, the lemon-lye, what with the acidic and the alkaline
muddling on into one odor,

he knew in his bones that the crescent-
moon would, for once, align
itself with the crescent-moon cut high in the long-gone outhouse door.

THE OLD WAYS

Peter Sansom   *Bluebell Wood*

We're no gardeners, me even less so,
going at our bindweed and stinging nettle,
the egg yolk suns of dandelions; till here,
in May, the lovely violet blush
of bluebells no-one planted. Bluebells
to bring back in their gouache mist
me and the dog, running, clodded furrows
giving way to Dumble Wood, and then the track

like a funnel into Bluebell Wood, in that
proud harriers vest, where we'd turn
in a curve for home through the lilac dusk
of harebell, wild hyacinth, wood hyacinth,
the furthest I'd been alone, me and the dog,
out to an arctic circle or timbuctoo
that everybody knew: 'You've been up Bluebell Wood?'

Then one year it was gone, just like that,
for a link road ten minutes quicker
to Mum's, to Tony's, to see Mick or Donald,
all of them, Auntie Olive, our Cynth, our Joss.
Bluebell Wood, right here, across the decades
of our garden, packed tight, and in among
is Dad, though he knew better, singing that
Bluebells are bluebells are blue bells are blue.

Joseph Allen   *Excavations*

The monotonous flow of lorries
over fallen snow.

These were meadows,
once we unearthed
broken clay pipes
close to the motte and bailey.

Hangings took place here,
Archer, the last,
A plague on the highway.

Headlights from the carriageway
filtering through snow,
non-stop deliveries,
trees creak in the wind
like a swinging rope.

Gillian Somerville-Large   *Emptying Seas*

One day we shall mourn
the white clad fishmonger
laying sopping flesh
on mottled marble
a sea in travesty;
one day we shall mourn
horseshoes of cod
nacreus herring
sulking John Dory
amber haddock
red veined roe
netted in membrane;
portions of whiting
dirty as old socks;
splayed mackerel striped
like tiger in front of
eastern sportsman;
flat fish wearing
seabed disguise,
sole, brill, turbot
plaice bright-dotted
black brother halibut,
crabs gathered in pans
dead as sunflowers;
round eyes, glass eyes, dead eyes
mad glare of hake,
sly glance of haddock
smashed ruby of herring,
cockeye of sole,
multiplied reproach
from heaps of sprats,
all that sea slaughter
all those dead fishes,
all that bounty
becoming a memory
of hovering flies
over skin and bones.

Gwyn Parry   *Welsh Confession*

We are responsible for chapels
empty of song and prayer.
We closed the big door,
turned off the electricity,
put the Bible on the shelf.
We let farms ruin,
their chimneys full of crows,
floors fallen with rot.
We destroyed the old customs
of spring, harvest and winter
by introducing the tractor.
We built roads to English cities
to bring an infection of caravans,
an invasion of the retired.
We depopulated the land,
made farmers shoot their dogs,
encouraged young men to take their lives
in smoke filled cars.
We pumped sewage and waste into the sea,
painted the insides of crabs black,
made fish grow eyes on their backs.
We have thrown away our oral tradition
and installed the television.

Brian Lalor

11

Margaret Moore   *Nancy*

When the boys were taken in turns to be frogmarched
through the Acts of the Apostles (Word made smog)
Juliet caps and panamas tilted forward
and the front row took silent flight for private heartlands.
My preferences were Camelot, Avonlea,
or on a Sunday after a Regal matinee
an airbase where every girl was a forces' sweetheart.

Even so when a collection hymn was in prospect
I'd tune half an ear to transmissions from Asia Minor
with the volume turned down, as halting East Antrim spondees
relayed journeys, conversions, endorsement of OT prophets
and scarier stuff.

They preached the resurrection.
A heavy text to us whose soles were green
from playing tig among headstones, leaping graves,
whose homecoming path sloped downward beside the churchyard.

When Nancy came, an evacuee from Belfast,
she brought a saving grace. Stuck by the teacher,
shaken out of fantasy mode, I longed to be sitting
inside the whispering zone where Nancy shared Smarties
and shared (I supposed) her village granny's secrets:
the use of pennies, bandages, strong-smelling lilies,
authorised rites for laying the restless dead.

MOTHERS AND FATHERS

Rita Ann Higgins   *Whitethorn*

Whitethorn is nearly covering Tuar Beag
a christening blanket with thorns.
When I see it I think of my mother's warning.

'Don't ever bring whitethorn into this house
for fear it would bring the mi-adh upon us
or on one of the youngsters not yet walking
but carrying their dividends of venial sin.'

Do ye renounce Satan? We do.

The force, with no name or place in this dimension
might drag one of them angels down with the fever
or some fierce shaking calamity.

Unseen with the naked eye
the force could take one half of the twins
down to the fairy fort or further into the fog
below Coyne's field, never to be seen again.

'The lord protect us from all harm
don't ever bring that whitethorn into the house.'

Do ye renounce Satan? We do.

Cate Huguelet *Boogeymen*

In case you are struck by a
moving car worse a moving truck
worse the bus that's meant to
carry you back and forth from
school in safety in case of random
bullets fired of razor-sharp icicles
loosened by the warmth of
winter's reprieve in case of
unexpected bouts of bubonic
yellow fever pox all sorts of
sinister viruses out of the reach of
antibiotic intervention in case of
the collapse of buildings and
bridges in case the ground
beneath your feet should shudder
and split with a terror and
violence that will haunt the
dreamlife of each and every
innocent bystander in case of
these things you must you must
you must remember to wear clean
underwear every time you leave
the house (i'm not saying god
does not cradle you in the palm of
his hand but each life you see
goes by in a blink of his eye just a
blink).

Nick Bridson Baker

14

Greg Delanty   *To My Mother, Eileen*

I'm threading the eye
            of the needle for you again. That is
my specially appointed task, my
            gift that you gave me. Ma, watch me slip this
                        camel of words through. Yes,
rich we are still even if your needlework
            has long since gone with the rag-and-bone man
                        and Da never came home one day – our Dan.
            Work Work Work. Lose yourself in work.
                        That's what he'd say.
                                Okay okay.
Ma, listen I can hear the sticks of our fire spit
            like corn turning into popcorn
                        with the brown insides of rotten teeth. We sit
in our old Slieve Mish house. Norman is just born.
            He's in the pen.
I raise the needle to the light and lick the thread
            to stiffen the limp words. I
peer through the eye, focus, put everything out of my head.
            I shut my right eye and thread.
I'm important now, a likely lad, instead
            of the amadán at Dread School. I have the eye
                        haven't I, the knack?
            I'm Prince Threader. I missed it that try.
                        Concentrate. Concentrate. Enough yaketty yak.
There, there, Ma, look, here's the threaded needle back.

Breda Spaight   *Making Butter*

Pacing the bright, tiled kitchen, you shake
the two-pint brown bottle in both hands –
a slosh-noise musical instrument in which you make
butter from the cream of our only cow.
A fly death-flays on the amber spiral of flypaper,
its hiss in tune with the listless drag of your heels.
You look exactly forward, seal-slick eyes
fixed on intimate history, a truth I pick from chaos.
I swam inside you once,
before which I lay in wait, no face,
– you, hymen-locked –
our purest time,
when everything between us
was dream, when I was as much of your parents,
and theirs, and you not yet hurt, or hurtful,
a daughter churning cream in wooden butter churns,
your body's rhythm in rhythm with your mother's,
and hers, a melody that instilled ovum-me
with an awareness of when music stops.

You poke butter blobs
through the bottleneck with a knitting needle,
scent of almond, dawn, wild garlic –
your eyes close, corpse-solid, 'Just for the taste.'

The fly, its wings outstretched, iridescent
in an angle of evening-pale light,
tranquil – poised for flight.

Ray Givans   *Mother to the Bride*

Those hands would knead a child's stooped head
as if applying carbolic along ribbed beads
of singing washboards, or stoking quagmires
of steaming clothes, doused in froth and suds,
while lip-reading through the steamie's fog
and chattering chorus.

Those hands would rise for you at 3 a.m., break
the ice, snap sticks, light the outhouse
boiler, stoke and pummel a mass of clothes
in a seething cauldron, peg and raise, criss-
cross a yard, enclosed, in shade. A wash
that flapped against the unction of dark clouds
slow moving over uniform tenements.

And now those hands grown gnarled, arthritic
have watched her body lose a pound each week
since the engagement. And yet, determined,
fumbling, drawing blood, she tacks the hem,
stitches and smooths with steaming iron
her daughter's gown.

Today, those hands will hold the shaking stem
of a champagne glass, watch the fizzing liquid
froth and bubble over the lip, consent to toast
her daughter's happiness, in a room ablaze
with starched white tablecloths.

A steamie was a public washhouse

Pamela Mary Brown　　　*Putting Out the Washing*

She felt the rain
brought the washing in
like a donkey carrying a creel on its hip
the bundle unacknowledged
the task an instinct

(to while away another moment
among scone bread necessities)

the rain came then
and she nodded to it
with spent workhorse eyes
that know the day will ebb
in the toil of getting on with life

hands worn clean
and feet routinely treading
to trample all trace of wonder
extract duty from love
until love itself is calloused
in the years that take all in the passing
even the sadness

those are her ghost moments in my memory
and I see her among forgotten generations of women
putting out the washing and bringing it in
putting out the washing and bringing it in
putting it out and bringing it in
until time falls
and night settles like a shawl to drape shoulders
that asked for nothing in the giving of themselves.

George Shorten *The Strong*

That dawn of a woman rose out of seaside bog.
The new road was down five years
When up she came with a blaze of face
Lurching and stooped and sixty at least
Counted change held hard
In one pocket of her kitchen coat
And a key.

She had smelt oils for an infant
Lifted limp from her bed.
Damp praying labours return
In her mother's dreams
Sundering screams to the woman who bore her.
She bled wordlessly for two long days
And a life.

Now she pulls up past the berry bushes
Aching with new fruit and the stubborn haw.
She hears the words of Paraic Colum
Just another aul' one's saw.
Her mind words form sentences with a clarity hard won
I have stayed busy the whole day long
I have cast off the weaknesses of motherhood
Like a summer shawl. I have been for my children
A place where they belong, a place where they can touch
The struggling strong.

Later the droves will move to mass
Down the hill to bow and bray
Pity the loss she'll hear them say
Pity the day.

John Daniel   *My Mother is a Ship*

My mother is a ship
let go, adrift on the open sea
so I shout to her about Sally
and Michael and the neighbours
but she's off
on the dark waters,
holding her head
as the craft bobs up and down
saying 'Thank you, thank you' to everything
while I pass around sweets to the others,
Nancy smiling as always,
Gwen taking her clothes off,
Jean telling everyone how she fought
in the Blitz, Doreen clutching
the wound in her thigh,
my mother rocking inside
the closed harbour of women
who have also been out and about—
kids, work, husbands,
mottled legs through which
babies have passed,
solitary anchors dropped
in the silt of the carpet
where the tv tolls in the corner
like a buoy
showing the way home.

Michael Laskey   *Visiting My Mother*

In the dazzle of arrival – their fluorescent
kitchen light flickering on, the groggy boys
extricated from their car seats and gently
propelled like toy boats across the pool
of gravel towards her, all the luggage
shuttled through – nappy bucket, Tim's blanket,
the dismantled travelling cot – and El Cid's
(treat it as a joke) when were we leaving? –
in the middle of all this, how she'd sometimes
stand still expectant somehow, perhaps
her hands slightly lifted from her sides
or her eyes a bit puzzled meeting mine,
and I'd realise I'd forgotten, no, worse,
that it hadn't even crossed my mind
to kiss her, so I'd hug her warmly at once,
only maybe just too late, much too late.

Geraldine Finn   *Waiting*

They sit together
In the front room
On the couch
And wait for
Christmas cheer to come

Their Madonna and Child
Silhouette
Is thrown onto the wall
By the on and off
Tree lights in the corner
And the frantic TV colours
That scream out
You've not bought enough yet

Her festive work is done
For now
The stuffed turkey
Lies in state
On the kitchen table
And Santa waits
On top of the wardrobe
Upstairs

She waits for the movie
To finish
Then leans across to him
And whispers
We'll eat now,
In case Daddy has been
Delayed again.

Hammond Journeaux

22

Maggie Harris   *Calling*

You're gone. A voice at the end of the line frizzling into night
rushing to ring off as usual (you never have any credit
and only have time to say what you phoned for)
I'm left cradling plastic and remembering the smell of you
all Johnson's baby and breast milk then later Charles Lauren
and I'm wondering how come time moved so fast from when I
first held a telephone – Uncle Bert's black Bakelite – 1966 age
twelve before my own migration and the mystery never left,
telephones and radios and how come a voice can crawl on
cables underneath the ocean and what's all that stuff about
sound waves and now satellites and look mum no hands smaller
and smaller mobiles
And now I'm thinking how quickly the words 'I'm mobile'
become 'immobile' with the removal of an apostrophe
remembering how you dropped your h's as quick as your skirts
rose, as quick as your new high boots would allow
And I think of you now in some city whose name I'm not
allowed to know, no longer linked by blood but stars
and the mystery returns
that absence of touch
cutting into my flesh like cheese wire

Eibhlín Nic Eochaidh   *Cradle Song*

I am your mother. Am not your mother.
Birthed you, nursed you, barely for three weeks.
Grown now, child to man. Raised by another.

The memory of you I pushed further
and further back. Key turned black.
I was your mother. Am not your mother.

Days I allowed myself remember
the crown of your head, curve of your cheek.
Grown now, child to man. Loved by another.

Times I lifted you from the bottom drawer,
memory box, nestled under cover of odd socks.
I am your mother; was not your mother.

The sentence using your name, said over
and over again to keep back the dark.
Grown now, child to man; your smiles for others.

Begin again. Say that when or ever
we meet, love is a presence unable to speak.
You, grown now, your life with others:
I am your mother and not your mother.

William Palmer   *Letter to My Daughter*

The hare limped trembling through the frozen grass ...

These words of Keats – the animal moving
through the vowels,
the consonants that stand
as frosted blades, or emptied trees

– I cannot give you any more than these –
 or, better – share them with you.
Their tenderness may make amends
for those harsh speeches, quickly uttered,

that seem to wither up the earth.
Our lives, our words –
they are the same. The one good gift
I'd give to you is knowing always

what I haven't always known myself
– that what's not given can never be returned,
that words, not given when they're sought
limp, tremble, rot into a frozen ground.

Philip Knox   *Saying*

breakfastbreakfast
this is a start bowlscupscoffee
good good this is good this is start
crumbs on table collecting in cracks
fossillising in cracks in table silent
crumbs – say it, just say it, look up and –
eyes burning already already it was the
bombshell so direct using me to get at
her i know that hurt i know but still
say it you have to say it you have to let
him know his eyes too burning a little too
red rims too – too much, too much, can't cry,
fall back, retreat, study orange juice, scan paper –

terroristbombingsthirteensuicidemurderbeckham

enough enough do it choke it out choke it out
can't even remember last time you said it
and he has to know now above all he needs to
know now when he feels he's all he has
crumbs crumbs more lines in his face today
his profile your profile his eyes yours
sun outside on the clouds above the fence you have to say it
bite toast steady nerves – how can it be so hard? –
saysaysay tear up this silence that's squatting
on your chest and saysaysay orange juice
tears in his eyes coffee grounds that old tree outside
with room still to grow say do it say –
'I love you. Dad.'

FAMILIES

Carol Rumens   *The Omen Bird*

She flew onto the fence of every yard
And garden of our youth and raised, thrush-throated,
Her rueful, mothering, mournful little cry:
True love, true love, it's not true love, admit it –
You'll never have true, true love like Dad and I!

Why think about it now? Leave her to fly
The winds or nest where memories are more sheltered,
More sheltering. If he and I wrong-footed
The marriage-dance, its tune was in our blood
And it was rock 'n' roll, not some old lie.
True love, true love, it's not true love, admit it –
You'll never have true, true love like Dad and I!

And if, one dawn, I walked out of his garden
Through mud and broken lifeless stalks, the dream
That lured me was an orchard of my own:
Lark-song was not more distant than that scream:
True love, true love, it's not true love, admit it –
You'll never have true, true love like Dad and I!

It's years, now, since we either loved or hated.
I'm dead to him. The orchard's down. So why,
Why does she perch on winter's crumbless ledge,
Her head one-sided with its bright tin eye,
Almost as if she saw our old pine bed
Still held the slumped conundrum, loosely knotted,
And she was trying to lure us from the edge:
True love, true love, it's not true love, admit it –
I'd never be surprised if you two parted!

Alan Brownjohn   *Theory of a Father*

'I can say that Darren has been different
Since he started seeing you,' his father says
To Maria, the Andorran meteo-chick.
'You must not be offended that I first thought
You might not be the best sort of influence.
But he has changed, and it must be due to you.'

Maria nods and smiles. 'I come,' she replies,
'From a little-known country to a well-known place.
Your Darren has been a firm location for me,
As I, I venture to think, may have been for him.'
(Though that last line she only thinks, doesn't say out loud.)
'And he's passed all of his subjects!'

'Seven A's,'
Replies the father, 'and one B which I believe
By rights should have been an A. In geography,
Which is his best subject. We shall appeal,
As you might expect.' And then he leaves
A very slight pause before he says, 'I notice
You are pregnant, by the way. The change of climate?'

A 'meteo-chick' is a young woman chosen to present
television weather forecasts as much because of her
appearance as for her meteorological knowledge.

Cherry Smyth *Other People's Money*

Saturdays were good in the counting room,
thumbed piles of a hundred, bound in a rubber
band, a sacrilege of biro on the top note;
the serious smell of coppers and leather,
ledgers transfiguring the departments below
into totals. I saw my father's exacting formality
in an aura of warm, slightly nervous, respect.
I counted so much of it, other people's money,
between 16 and 18, exposed to its quiet,
concentrating fever, I gained an immunity.

Later, my father, long retired, sits me
and my mother at the kitchen table, presents
his money files, his dockets, his policy numbers
and tries to transfer their knowledge to us. We
nod vigorously, ask questions that reveal how little
we've understood, like a telephone pole trying
to talk to a leaf. He becomes skittish, angry
and in time, the three of us are in tears. Not
because there isn't enough, but because Dad won't
believe and Mum and I can't get the decimal
points in line. We're stuck in this balance sheet,
desperate to make out our own bodies, somehow
put them together again. My father cries *it's hopeless.*

We coax him back to things we can handle, things
he's provided, the cup, the saucer, the plastic tumbler.
And all around him we can sense the years he can't
be sure of, how many, how much, and the not
knowing has broken him loose, jangling. My mother
and I know nothing, have never known. 'We'll manage
you know,' we say. 'We've always managed.'

Gregory O'Donoghue   *Sibling*

                           For Dave

Mother came home
showing off my brother –
I bided time
until it was alone,

fed it a sandwich
of clay and worm,
privet leaves for bread;
the brat survived.

So goes family legend
yet, now and then,
I am inclined
to re-imagine

that sandwich a gauche
manner of greeting –
clueless go at communing
with the creature.

Kevin Graham   *Gemini*

I can picture my viscous torso
being scooped like a prize
into a white nest of coddled towels,
nostrils flaring in the all-too-quick air,
its release a map of panic and sudden sky,
belly pushing up, squeezing in,
lungs whirring into autopilot,

as natural to the open world
as a terrible minute later
when they coaxed my lifeless twin,
limp from asphyxiation,
more bloody-blue than pink,
and in the silence I couldn't have known
was the memory of his foot

trailing mine, assuring me
that although life may not unfold
the way the river shucks its load,
its colours would hold the key
to these rooms of dreamless white:
my older brother, in his infant wisdom,
must have sensed me leaving first –

the cord gripping his baby-neck –
and tapped me on the ankle
to let me know there'd be a time when,
hunched over the side of the bed,
I'd be wrestling with a sock
and my heart would dip like a robin,
and I'd know, just know.

Joan Jobe Smith   *Are You Lonesome Tonight?*

After my black Irishman husband drank cognac
and listened over and over on the hi-fi to Elvis
sing 'Are You Lonesome Tonight?' he'd
come to bed and weep and I'd hold him in
my arms the way I did our children and I'd
pat his shoulders, say there-there and he'd
tell me again the story his mother told him
of the night his father beat her and then
kicked her 8-months pregnant belly so hard
it killed the other baby inside her, his twin
brother who'd been born stillborn, and he'd
tell me how all his life he missed his brother
and wondered what he'd've been like: would
they've both played baseball, liked to fish,
loved the same girl, bought a black Corvette?
The dead baby, his stillborn twin, his mother
told him was the spitting image of him and
while he grew up she always said when he
didn't like school, drank vodka at 15, got
fired from jobs, wrecked his Corvette: thank
God there was only one of you. They often say
that when there are twins there is sometimes a
Good twin and a Bad twin and how could he
ever know which one he was and this sorrowful
obligato, this aria of pathos only Elvis a twin
too could understand as they sang together,
their voices twin tenors: 'Are you lonesome
tonight?' a hymn, a prayer, a solemn promise
to repair the wound, replace the heart and soul
that died that night in his mother's womb,
if not in reality, then surely in eternity.

Eugene O'Connell   *Rylane*

I saw him once in the place of the rumour
of how he waited for a dead brother to step
off a bus, a place that had a weather of its
own, an atmosphere that clung to it like grief.
I didn't know him personally and now he's
gone can only guess at what possessed him
to squat all those years under a furze bush
that dripped on to his clothes. Maybe he
did know and didn't let on, since he had
no other interests, decided to play to the
gallery, ham it up for the prying eyes of
passengers who'd warmed to his notoriety.
The legend of the man who waited in the back
of beyond for a bus to bring his brother home.

Desmond O'Grady   *Grandson*

You open your day, our lives, as the lead actor
his theatre. Welcomed, you're prepared for today's
performance with women's talk. Disrobe. Pose with pleasure,
then don the costume tailored for your new play's
old story and stroll out on your stage reflects our world.
We play to your gestures, plain or purled.

Your first act's set in spring green garden sunshine
where you delight in the morning's comedy with reclined
waves, held gasps, small smiles. Your orchestration.
The players in your park respond in kind.
A pal or dog you grant men's talk attention,
but your sight's set on grander satisfaction.

Lunch, like newspapers, serves prescribed plates of talk,
that three course play within the play. You sit
up to and hold table with each remark.
Eat well, then have something to show for it.
Afternoon, like history, gives pause for reflection
on life's confusion and its safe solution.

Nightfall. Your bath is drawn after you dine
so you may wash away your day's distractions.
Then you both plot. She with her glass of wine,
you with your bottle, like two gay tragedians.
Darkness beds you. Sound sleep brings on those dreams,
nightmares that act out your still small boy's schemes.

Rhiannon Shelley   *For Cian Tadhg Gabriel*

'I can't know the words' you say today,
grasping at the air, 'I missed them.'

And I lost the right ones long ago,
my eternal poet of the mountain,
but crushing and boom crashing
into my own existence of exile,
of absences, silence and loss,
rushes that rosy blood bloom flush this
warm blush of love, your presence.

So let me tell you these words, this day,
my own child and so much your own; let me
make a present of your history to you:

a small and sunlit back garden by
the sea, your sand blown hair lifting
in the jasmine breeze and I see darkening
after four astonishing years of our lives;
your laughter helter skeltering a clothesline
white washing your new expression freshly
brushing a sky slanting clear speaking clean corn
flower blue and tomorrow, these days of tomorrows

that you will one day forget. The years shall
hush these moments, so listen my darling,
my only baby boy: the words that I can give you,
the only ones worth knowing, are about the joy
from which you came, my love, and the love
to which you will always, now, be going.

Michael Longley   *The Wren*

I am writing too much about Carrigskeewaun,
I think, until you two come along, my grandsons,
And we generalise at once about cows and sheep.
A day here represents a lifetime, bird's-foot trefoil
Among wild thyme, dawn and dusk muddled on the ground,
The crescent moon fading above Mweelrea's shoulder
As hares sip brackish water at the stepping stones
And the innovative raven flips upside down
As though for you. I burble under your siesta
Like a contrapuntal runnel, and the heather
Stand that shelters the lesser twayblade shelters you.
We sleepwalk around a townland whooper swans
From the tundra remember, and the Saharan
Wheatear. I want you both to remember me
And what the wind-tousled wren has been saying
All day long from fence posts and the fuchsia depths,
A brain-rattling bramble-song inside a knothole.

George Szirtes   *A Lead Soldier*

The soldier was the first thing he could weigh
In his closed palm and feel somehow assured.
He watched it as it watched him where he lay,

Knowing he might endure what it endured.
Being a child he was aware of childhood,
Knowing the cell in which he was immured

And all the rules of being bad and good.
His nails ran round the soldier's form, the face,
The back of the knee, the plinth on which it stood

Ready to venture, glaring at a space
Behind the wardrobe or the enemy
Propped by the ink pot, where it had the grace

A child lacks, having no autonomy.
Even inside its box with others
It held its posture with economy.

It was like having regiments of brothers
Each more valiant than the last, a palette
Of reds and blues. The child was light as feathers,

Too vulnerable. He needed an amulet
To see him through the nights his parents fought.
The soldier was the rough weight of a bullet,

A boiled-down heart, like his, more finely wrought.

Joakim Säflund

Frances Cotter   *News*

Sun spanned
the family room.

Mother hummed
as she dusted
faces in frames.

The dog lay
panting slightly.
Occasionally,
his tail thumped.

Father sipped tea,
reading the deaths.
Firewood spat,
the radio murmured.

Distorted
in the frosted glass
two guards.

When he opened
the door, blue
tinged the room.

She gripped the last photo.
'Which one of them is it?'

Tom Duddy   *The Callers*

You cannot trust them, these mild-
mannered callers who flow
past you into your parlour,
tossing your snow globe
without waiting for the storm,
inclining their head to read
the spines of your faber & fabers.
You are afraid for your child.
You are afraid to leave them
alone with your child, knowing
they practice only one virtue.

You go upstairs at your peril.
On your way back to the parlour
you will find your child standing
dazed at the threshold of the hall.
What have they said to her? What part
of her life have they grazed
with their casual love of the truth?
Did they discover her first still-life
folded beside the glass elephant,
fielding flies on the window sill?

All evening, not knowing when
they will try for the truth again,
you agree with nothing they say,
till their faces are pale and drawn,
and they sit with their hands loosely
joined, waiting for the cars to come.

BIRTH

Leland Bardwell   *Inish Murray*

* *An áit in a mbíonn bó, bíonn bean,*
agus an áit in a mbíonn bean bíonn miotún

Two thumb holes in the birthing stone,
beside the women's graveyard.
There she squats, prayers
breaking from parched lips
to the great Mangod to deliver her
from the yearly gall of labour.
To beg for a manchild
to erase the guilt of her sex.
For being a woman
has no pardon.
Skirts raised in the wind,
on an island that floats
like a bay leaf
in the unforgiving sea,
she crouches thus
till the infant lies in the scutch.
And she looks at the unmarked grave
beneath whose soil
her mother lies,
and ponders.

* *'Where there is a cow there is a woman and*
where there's a woman there's mischief.'
– St Columcille, who founded the
monastery and banned all cows from
the island.

'Sheela' by Denise Hogan

Daphne Rock   *Saint*

Whispers insistent in her ear all spring – even before she knew, before
cells tucked under her heart doubled and doubled again...
this one is mine.

This one is mine, oblate, given into charge of holy men.
Whispers, catching her sharply there in the womb, no matter,
She was only a vessel, soon to be emptied.

Doctors do not hear voices. They would cut and stitch, she would be
good as new, almost, might even conceive again
with this one out of the way.

Whispering drowned other sounds, cribs being draped and vests knitted,
people painting the room in yellow and blue,
the talk of names.

This one is mine, even the seed head buried in the ovum
is fit for Paradise...Perhaps she still (weakening now, illness sapping her)
expected miracles.

Whispering in the shawl's folds, the child calls *mother, mother*
but the saint is silent, there is only the whisper of rain
falling in the churchyard.

*In memory of the woman who was
canonised by the then Pope because she believed that to
have a life-saving operation which would kill the
child she was carrying would be a sin.*

Kevin Crossley-Holland

Miriam
(born on Monday, August 16th, 2010)

I have entered the garden of superstition
where it is unwise to gaze at moon jellyfish
or the undersides of toadstools
and a scuff on the bracelet bearing your name
may be no less a portent
than a crack in the teacup or temple.

Fairy godmothers and Fortune herself
are not so much inevitable as invited.
I am in league with prime numbers,
hagstones and anagrams – even the lottery –
and potter about, smelling lavender.
I consort only with whatever is propitious.

Each day I am learning more
about longing and the longed for,
attending to my Hebrew.
I have met your half-sisters,
Maria and Mariam, Minnie, Maire,
and I kneel before the Virgin.

Etymology has its limitations.
Your name like all names grows in sound:
the humming of bees, vowels cheeping,
and that capricious *r*, rolled in the throat
or butterfly light, fluttering on the tip
of the tongue. That's the sum of it.

Billy Ramsell   *Gabriel's Waltz*

It is said that the philtrum, the indentation between the nose and the
upper lip, is made by the finger of the angel Gabriel as he comforts
each child at the moment of its entrance into this world

Sssh. My finger on your lips
and my finger tracing your tears
is not quite enough
to shut you up

as you whimper,
as you sob out your terror
at these strange shores you've surfaced on, dripping,

as if you can already sense the barbarians
that lurk behind bushes,
at the head of the classroom,
like wraiths down back alleyways,
behind a certain percentage of neighbourly faces.

God knows how many times I've been through this.

Right now you're just a bundle of futures
all of them featuring whiteness, sneezes, somebody's hands,
alarms that scream for attention,
stray light, sleep's mud bath,
a corn-coloured dress among the barley,
a piano, abandonment, light collapsing.

Let's get it clear from day one that you're here for life.
All that's uncertain is the long or the short of it.
And may you not leave it as you entered,
in a hospital ward in the dead of night
after panting and hard labour...

Hush. Stop whining now.
It's just headlights slanting through the window,
the night nurse yawning on her rounds.
A door slams in the corridor. Machines beep.

Welcome home.

Hilary Elfick   *Moment of Birth*

As if this were a normal birth he announced it,
laughing, so they all filled up their glasses
under sagging bougainvillea where
bleached butterflies were darting, hiding
from the mynahs' shriek and clatter, and
the glasses clinked, the sky grew green,
and Brett came over, slapped him on the back

which meant they all uncorked more wine
while in that crowded, bubbled, lazy twilight
on our neighbour's terrace I just stood there
seeing only this frail child, too light for life to bear
inside translucent skin too thin to take the
needles and the probes, her sticky mouth so
tiny for the finest filament of oxygen and formula

and you there, you my darling child,
so drained, so pumped tight with your fresh
four pints of borrowed blood, straining to
see her spread out flat through all that bottled glass,
so thick, so brittle and so crossed with
wires, she who should have been
too small to shout, but shout she did
before they swept her from your streaming thighs;
so Mark outside the unit strained his panicked ears,
trying to guess which one of you had cried
and whether either of you'd ever cry again

and then that short rush he had made to find
a phone and race like Puck a half way round the world
to say that she'd been born which then had made your
father come back out with sparkling wine,
lift up his laughing glass and no one under all those
crimson flowers, picking at fat oysters and hot
mussel fritters, stopped to ask why ever we were
laughing in December all those months too soon,
and whether it was safe to raise our glasses
to our end-of-day euphoria except that somehow
all she was, so tiny, so yet unreal, so unsure
of her next breath, still had the right, the right,
the right to such a celebration as this.

Jeanette McCullough

GROWING UP

Frank Dullaghan   *Blanket*

Now he's normal again, he forgets
that summer turning brown
and the edge of ice in the breath of morning,
means the college term begins
and he must begin,
repeating his disrupted year,
must face new faces and wait
for them to think him odd,
wandering up the field alone
at lunch-time to eat his sandwiches,
where the only close sound
is the sound of the grass kissing the breeze,
there and there and there,
and where his mind can follow
its own tune and settle
into the comfort of that rhythm
and not think about the instructions
his art teacher gave
for his *Journeys* project
or how she couldn't see
that this had to be about a mad scientist
taking control of every mind
by pointing his insane machine
and how the only safe place
to think this through is the field,
where the earth can rise around you
like a blanket of love
that shuts out the glare of the world.

Jim Conwell *The Day After*

Of course you understand he wants something but what for Chrissake?
I never could figure it out and I defy you to either.
He just hangs around with something he doesn't say dripping off him.
We feed him his tea
and he spends most of the time wandering about,
sometimes playing as if nothing else in the world existed.
'Dreaming', that's the only word for it.
I think, sometimes, the fairies took him out there in the bottom field.
I've seen them there once or twice as evening was falling.
They do be careful but sometimes you can spot them.
They took him off somewhere and when he came back sure
it was as if some small part of him was missing.
What part would that be? Well I'd be hard-pushed to put a name to it now.

If I sit in here, with my back against the bank,
careful not – like some city fool – to sit among the pismires,
I can stop and think. It is quiet and no-one is around.
If they find me here, they'll want me to come along.
I hear the sound of a bucket put down on a rock.
Maybe they're feeding the calves.
In the house, women make bread, or butter.
Things stir in me, constantly on the move, shuffling and pushing for space.
If it can remain unspoken, there is no end to what I understand.

Gary Allen   *That Summer*

The yards slipped away to shadow
came to the point of all creation
the dust on border bluebells
on the flower heads of rhododendron bushes
the toad carried from the damp corner
exposed and left to dry out in the fierce sun
after all, we were Gods, cruel in our discoveries
the cracked bedding pots and roof slates
the opaque windows of the sheds
the dowel-rods of the humming pigeon lofts
the green park beyond the walls
where men in pee-smelling trousers
put you to sleep:
everything changed that afternoon
Gods took on the image of mortals
as the heat sapped all strength
as wasps sunk into death in water filled jam jars
the back bedroom curtains pulled shut
no one told us to be quiet
no one warned us to stay in the yards
if there was crying, it was softer
than the splutter of a car on the straight road
running black between two points to the coast –
that was the summer we metamorphosed
into something other than Gods
that summer whole streets of houses burned
crackled in the blistering heat
stones cut into flesh, families fled estates
as we waited quietly on the steps
long past the hour of supper.

Ted McCarthy   *St Anne's*

The pencil, pared to a spear-point,
snaps at the application of a thought.
Morning is over, all that remains of its promise
is a varnished press, a wall of faces
looking out from various faded summers:
my grandfather, kindly, sitting by the flowerbeds
we avoided like fire – my aunt's scalding voice
warning against football; children by a rockery,
a ghost hovering above the lens...

long days, the lawn smothered by daisies,
strawberry nets unfurled, tented on twigs.
Outside now, nature – old men on seats
mystified by what they've missed,
garden becoming field; our paths
no longer what they were. And the old hunger
still, something of the boy burning, a kick
of desire that can never be released,
a sadness at the height of summer.

Maybe, above all, we mourn the death
of tidiness, that moment, fixed in the mind,
when everything was relative, when the stars
were less even than their names,
and knowledge was a sea, not deep,
too far away to hem us in. And why
I have been running in my head
after an afternoon that never happened.
It has been a diving into dark

in hope of next day's dawn, a long forgetting
of things that can never be touched,
objects that become remote as mountains.
It is an ancient snare, that wish to be like Christ
ascending into his memories; to move and breathe
in a stainglass world, lucent, radiant. I trace
the cold rim of a bell, I run my hand
along a picture-frame, and find myself
suddenly blessed by its dust.

Eiléan Ní Chuilleanáin   *Desire*

I might go back to the place
Where I was young. This wide terminal city
– And I've lived so much longer here –
Fills up with corners; 1 turn.
All I have done combines to excavate
A channelled maze where I am escaping.

Now that the colours begin
Greying and fading before the doors even
Close, the graffiti are losing
Such savour as they owned;
The new road masks the glimpse of a church door.
On the philanthropic flats high gables freeze

Behind the baked red frieze
Where the date in flourished figures gathers
A cloak of soot around it
And does not want to be looked at:
The floating curls melt away; the flowing hands
Curve, do not grasp, not quite; the paid line

Almost lost quivers, there still,
As a child going off down a hill
Turns at the curve of a crescent,
Dissolving in light, in the view
From where her aunt sits marking her piebald
Galleys on her porch: turns again, and shouts goodbye.

LOVE, ONE TO ONE

Edward Power   *First Love*

Shouts in the macho schoolyard
Ambushed all my silences; now
Like down from the breast of lost echo,
Stillness drifts around me. I've come back
To look for one whose whispers hid
Amidst the swagger-talk of rougher lads.
I remember. I try.
But it's as hard now to picture him
As it was at first to catch his eye.

Sometimes standing side by side
We'd let our hands touch, or our thighs
Enjoy the moment till we feigned surprise.
Because weren't we, after all, two boys
In perfect working order: acting our ages:
Sometimes I'd be twenty
And he my Greek young thing.

We loved to send our voices
Crashing into hillsides
Or catch kingfisher's wink of blue
From the bridge-eye. Girls
Were of another paradise.
We fished here
Shared rod and glances
Caught our own reflections
Desire was enigma
Wrapped in shyness
Wild bog iris
Waved its sex
To every passing breeze.

O my young saint.
This is where the sun drowned
And the moon was born.
Stream's an opaque trickle now.
Cattle shit in the shallows,
Drink our mirror dry.

Celia de Fréine   *Let Him Skip Hence*

What if I was enamoured of an ass –
Oberon had become a bore of late
and when he started on those same crass
jokes and tiresome stories I couldn't wait

to head for my neck of the wood, little
thinking he'd trail behind like a lovesick
schoolboy, smear me with oxalic spittle
aided and abetted by that side-kick

of his. I'll have any sprite I fancy
wherever and whenever I like. Rue
the day I met the wretch. He'll not bring me
to heel. I could tell you a thing or two

about that night of unbridled passion –
only such deeds have gone out of fashion.

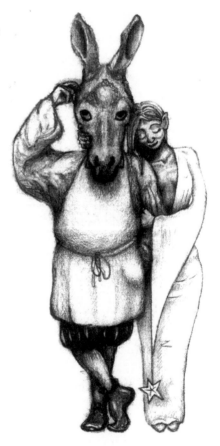

Theo Wakeman

52

Brian Mackey   *Rejudgement*

If the air were being harvested of wheat
It would strike like this
Tapered yellowing friable sunlight
Up and down the street.

The speed and dazzle of the day
Makes it easy to announce her to himself.
He could, if he were crazy, look away;
Sense her merely from the circumstance.

He stays in the doorway
And she goes by with slow total consequence,
Aware perhaps of being seen as the centre of the world,
Electrons everywhere in orbit around her.

And taking the light deliberately,
Slackly;
Feeling entitled to a proper setting
Or some sort of harsh justice that she might ignore.

It will be as if by returning to a door
That he will remember this summer;
What he makes of it,
Light when she has gone
Bearing and scattering his sight of her.

Ann Dean   *Merrion Square Snow Flurries*

I leave the reading
my mind over heated,
running on
what was said
and what was sung
between the listeners,
the poet
and the lutenists.

On Nassau Street
your absence
is an ice crystal
on my right shoulder
between me and the traffic.

I go into Hanna's, ponder
three for the price of two,
novels I won't read, pass
shelves of classics
into darkness,
and you are there again
a ticking in my head

but I'm focused
on poetry tucked in shadow,
bring it into snow-light
turn pages, think of you,
know exactly where you are
and what you're doing at 2.30pm.
You elude me like thinning ice.

I walk through slush
catch the bus, finger
print in my pocket.
Through misted windows
your absence is wordless
language the poets make presence
singing for both.

Helena Nelson   *Leap Year*

With my little eel, he said,
I could make electricity between your thighs.
Size, he alleged,
had nothing to do with it.
He was at his peak.
It was a matter of technique.

When he said 'thighs,' I thought of loins.
When I thought of loins I imagined chops
sitting in metal trays in butchers' shops.
Not the right image, clearly.

Quite often I have nearly
got into a sticky situation
but my pristine reputation
has extended into my prime
because of the way I leap
to the wrong connotation
or the wrong rhyme.

It happens all the time.

Jeanette McCullough

Eileen Sheehan   *Trespass*

I would lead you
by the bone
of your finger

to my bed
at the top
of the house

if now
was our time

but another's flesh
holds you

still a warm wind
flows round me

like the dream
of a life
we once shared

and if time is a wheel
then earth
will not hold us

until then
I am the shell that retains
you are the sound of the sea

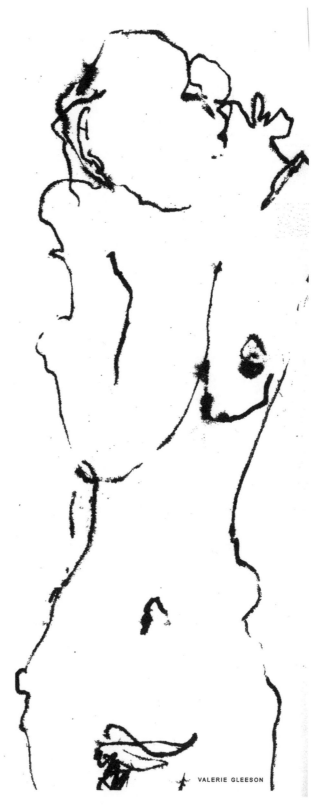

Valerie Gleeson

Michael Curtis   *Chiaroscuro*

Still out there
where three stars meet the night
where the last ferry
traces its just visible wake
to make the capital by nightfall

still out there
the half-moon, clouded, resisting light
aching for chiaroscuro
for the black and white definitions
our planets sometimes allow us

where happiness brightens
burns off what we no longer need
as we take or leave
the quiet, the desperate lives
the high seriousness of consumption

and let love remind us
to set aside the list
abandon the diary, the note
scribbled on the kitchen wall
knowing we'll remember what we must

letting triangulated planets
shuffle and dispose their brilliance
stretch and shrink tonalities
indulge our better selves
show the way to the last ferry.

Deborah Moffatt   *Swans on the Road*

There were swans on the road when I woke at dawn,
A road the swans had mistaken for a river, black water gleaming.

Or perhaps it wasn't water at all, or a road, but the dark morning sky,
And what I had taken for swans were small white clouds drifting by,

While all the time you slept inside the darkened room, your head
A shadow on the snowy pillow, your beating heart calling me back to bed,

But when I went to lie beside you the sheets were icy cold,
And the sound I had mistaken for your beating heart

The beating wings of the swans rising from the road,
Flying off before the gathering storm.

Ian Harrow   *Conversation*

When you pour wine from your glass into mine
to prolong the conversation so that what we are
together trying to say will materialize, I can see
that friendship has survived everything marriage
has thrown at it. We must die alone, we agree,
though I for one secretly hope this is so much talk.

Matthew Wakeman

Kevin Higgins   *No Reflection*

Since you left,
        the upstairs toilet
has developed what sounds like
        indigestion.
The cooked chicken
        I bought last night said to say
it's missing you.
        The cockatiel
escaped its cage just now,
        went out the window
shrieking: 'I don't know what I want
        but this isn't it.'
The doctor called.
        According to his records,
technically,
        I'm dead.
He told me: 'Look in the mirror';
        and when I wasn't there
said if you don't come home
        immediately, I may never
see me again. Hope
        you're enjoying your holiday.

Vona Groarke   *We Had Words*

Another hurricane, the third this month, strikes at the heart
of a city far from here. Tomorrow, its leftovers will fill our drain
and leak into the basement to advance on our low-tide mark
a seepage shot with grit and aftermath. My sleep tonight
will be a skimming stone affair: every hour fulfilling an ellipsis
predicted by the last. This day, all day, is hypothetical.
When it gives itself up to an offhand dusk, not even I will
muster a send-off beyond the thought of dust in darkness,
a breathless stowaway, like your words on the flip side
of my tongue, one almost completely slipped inside another.
I was saying, likening the way you like to single out
a single word to bear the weight of this, to boarded windows
and spineless pines bent double in thin air; cars afloat
on streets that have lost the run of themselves by now;
a casket in a clutch of branches, an item of clothing
tied to a T.V. aerial, for help. It bypasses us completely.
Your full leg, white as that whip-lashed shirt, has drifted
over mine. A siren flares on the pike. It plays itself out
in hours perched on high ground; our breath brimming over;
our new words islanded and arch, to steer us wide of harm.

Luis Fanti

David Page   *Bus and Bird*

And you did take that bus. I saw it go
so many more times. I can see it still
pull up and stop and leave. How could I know
if you had gone for good, or gone for ill?

Parted a quarter century ago,
right now we hurry to the window-sill
to watch our barn-owl glide on the meadow
pallid, unhurried, waiting for the kill.

Actions freeze into images just so
to keep alive our anguish, or to thrill.
This, in the end, is what we have to show:
a bus that would not wait, a bird that will.

Julia Dale   *Penelope*

the sky was simple to undo –
  one pull, and out it ran
in crimpled filaments of blue;

my fingers picked the ocean's span
  to nothing – mountains, too,
    in sudden mists
  of loosened thread
  dissolve, slip to my feet
and all those distances
travelled with such risk
  and such resolve
    unravel
      in
      little
  heaps

how small the world has grown –
  as darkness shrinks
from its bare loom the earth

I pause: something minutely sewn
  on this last patch of ground –
    one white
    flower
but time's not mine – once found,
  the petals,
    leaves, this
      single
      shred

are picked apart, night's edges fray,
  and, there, out starts the sun
weaving its hours across the day:

  I gather, and begin.

Enda Coyle-Green   *Your Hands*

What is the problem here –
is it the light, the light
of early spring, of early autumn,
or the grey air and the blue sky
compressed
into the last flat gasp
of day?

What are we talking about here –
is it the trees, bent down, heads hard
against the breeze, or the rush
into green, the rush
into evening,
your hands on the wheel,
the miles?

What are we frightened of here –
is it the sky, like a bowl
overturned on the earth,
the stars spilt
the stars hard and unyielding,
the cold night
and a terrible silence?

Sinéad Morrissey   *Adultery*

It is exactly a year today since you slapped me in public.
I took it standing up. You claimed I just ignored it,
that I pretended to be hooked on the dumb-show of a sunset,
splashing, a mile off. Too hooked to register
the sting of your ring finger
as it caught on my mouth and brought my skin with it.

All the next day I rolled with a migraine
down a merciless gallery that was mercifully without sun.
Sloshed tea in the saucer when your name came up.
I couldn't stop the cup of my hurt
flowing over and over until I saw there was no end of it
and only an end to me. How promiscuous pain can be.

He gave me roses. The surprise of butterflies caged in the palms.
And letters with hundreds of juvenile crosses, scented with sandalwood.
All of which I kept. One of which, leaked.
The truth – that you never were so solid or so huge
as the second his writing stumbled out of my pocket
and into your hands – got dropped between us like a fallen match.

You turned away as the sun disappeared like a ship. And I,
suddenly wanting to be struck again, to keep the fire of your anger lit,
I bit my lip.

Ita O'Donovan   *'And I Pronounce You Separate Man*
                      and Separate Woman'

And the nights when the moon and stars were not only right but colliding;
and the four warm bundles, snuggle-eyed, groaning, each in turn
a mighty wonder;
and my exhausted head on your lap and you caressing it when the last
fledgling had tucked his under wing;
and the day all the wellingtons were left on the island strand like tree
stumps from a sunken forest, and you bending, oars lifting and
dripping, as we rowed back in silence;
and the day you went fishing with my brothers, they having helped you
first to paint the house, and the singing over the water as the engine
putted home, but with no salmon in the boat;
and the screeching rush to casualty, I holding Mickey's limp body, his
eyelids fluttering and our hopes rising as we reached the gates;
and your mother and sister holding the fort when we flew to Paris, a
blue hazed city that called out to all our joyful senses;
and I polishing my grandmother's brass candlesticks for your father's wake;
and my sister's anniversary party when a tumbling brood of youngsters
as alike and unlike as pebbles on a beach, twelve cousins, sang and danced for us.
Mo croidhe geal gaor, death would have been the easy parting.
Now there is the slow painful picking apart of the strands of our life,
the warp and now the weft.
Before I take hold of the dreaded spear of Scawtha with its thirty
sharp-wounding heads or put a *geas* on you, here, let us take the needle and
unpick that last thread.

> *Mo croidhe geal gaor:* My bright heart close to me, my dearest one
> *geas*: a prohibition, magically imposed
> 'The spear of Scawtha': Scawtha was a prophet and a great warrior.
> She had the training of Cuchulainn for a year and a day,
> and gave him the invincible spear, the *gea bulga*.
> (Unless he got it from Aoife, as some accounts have it.)

Louis Mulcahy   *The Lighthouse*

I have seen the flashing light at night
come beam across the bay.
I have seen ghost ships sail in at dawn
slide out again at dusk.

I have seen the cranes ease up their loads
and smoothly set them down.
I have heard big lorries blaring horns
behind their engines' tune.

Then I know that on its way
a pallet bears a box
with written clearly over it
your address in my hand.

I wish that you could take your hurt
and place it in that box
to send its burden here to me
where I would need no crane

to take it in my arms
hoist it to my back
bear it for you evermore
through years of falling light.

John McKeown   *Morning Sickness*

Sick with desire this morning
the sunlight long with the years
of wanting you.

Your face in my mind
like the dust in the sunbeams
regrouped reformed
different from yesterday
but the same.

The years get longer
since you were the source
but I think at death's door
they'll reach me and stir me
and I'll pass through

still sick for want of touching you.

Robert Hamberger   *On the Prom*

On weekend mornings we walk beside the sea,
ready to face the air, unlatched from work,
turning to watch the way the sky shakes free.

Pearly blues cloud over us, to be
loosened into weather while we talk.
On weekend mornings we walk beside the sea.

Thank you for sleeping near me,
adding a word, a hand, when bad dreams break,
turning to watch the way the sky shakes free.

Are we settling here? Our choice rose simply,
like an answer, a top-hatted man on a bike.
On weekend mornings we walk beside the sea.

Joggers puff past. Seven waves lazily
flop their lines of white, shrugging before they strike,
turning to watch the way the sky shakes free.

I catch the sun. You're stretching like a tree.
Softer than sparrows, before the pier's awake,
on weekend mornings we walk beside the sea,
turning to watch the way the sky shakes free.

Beverley Gene Coraldene

70

Neil Bedford   *Jacmanii*

Early spring we bought clematis
expecting it to bloom in May
climb trellis with gusto but
it just sat there greenly
not unhealthy not unsick
just greenly enjoying the south facing
we'd set it in, advisedly.
You fed it, watered it although
that summer of showery sunshine
water was no problem
and now in October it explodes
into purple glory
just when we thought
the year was over.

I am growing in love with you
after gentle exchange of roots
tendrils searching for sustenance
hesitant connections
reinforced by scarcely visible ties.
The flowering so unexpected
Overdue
Takes me by surprise
An autumn riot
when we should be settling down
to log fires
and the quiet evenings of our age.

LIVES

Sebastian Barker   *Autobiography*

I waded in the shallows, watching sticklebacks.
Later, at school, I learnt how to compose
Sticklebacks out of words and numbers
To set them free in the river of my mind.

Later, the oceanography of water
Came in handy, as I sailed
The world, a water-boatman on the globe
Of unfathomable reason.

The world, too true, was tricky,
But the one inside me more so.
So I drank the wine of oblivion,
A familiar face in every port.

One day, in the mirror, I saw myself,
A composition of words and numbers,
Broken blood vessels and grey hairs.
So I said to myself, It's time to be off.

And out on the long river of my mind
I sailed to you on the tremendous
Oceanography of the sea
Outside myself, you graced on the quay at dawn.

Patrick Galvin   *Lost John*

Under this stone lies Lost John
He was strange as anyone

I am Lost John
I have no face
I belong to no race
Lost John
Of no place.

I was born of loss and dree
No breast to tender me
Those who made me were shorn
Those who named me, soon gone.
I am Lost John.

I make rivers of blue stone
Looking-glass of skin and bone
But I never can see
Where Lost John should be –
Tell me.

I walk with knobbled stick
No roof or bed of tick
No mark of where I've been
No lake to wash me in.
I am Lost John.

I look on God's face
I ask of him a place.
What I see in men's eyes –
Is naught but lies.

I sleep in harrowed ground
No bones of me be found.
She who buried me not known
He who bartered me has flown.
I am Lost John.

Patrick Moran   *Ferment*

To have lived for years like this.
Recalling – unable to forget –
the still unravelling drama of abuse:
sandal-squeak at midnight; his fag-stained breath;
that unspeakable release.

To have lived for years like this,
each new day the spectre of yesterday.
Crumbling, shell-like, in a lover's embrace.
Numbing pain and shame with booze. Brooding,
brooding; waiting for grace, or ease.

To have lived for years like this,
never quite able to say it out...
Just sporadic splutterings, oblique tirades.
A spasm of fists flailing at shadows.
Wounds reopening. Splintered glass.

Denise Garvey   *Spark*

Born into a house of *shalt, shalt not*
fish for Friday, starched teatowels
meat and two veg.
I stepped out into the air of *maybe, maybe not*,
ironed my clothes, but not my socks,
though starched sheets were delivered weekly
like Mass on Sunday. I cooked bolognaise.

I stretched into wonder,
stitched bed linen into decorations,
voted Conservative, striked with Labour
watched a gold slung sheik sneer
at women, like me, doing technical degrees.
I prayed with Protestants,
partied with Persians, spoke Farsi.

I climbed into machines to hide
from staring eyes that wondered what
a woman with a spanner could do in overalls ?
Crocheted babypink bonnets for mechanics' children,
cried at the layoffs, bussed my way home
in oily clothes, and washed up, baked
birthday cakes in the shape of trains.

Using a pick, crampons and ropes, I broke through
an ice ceiling, then slipped in an avalanche,
smothered in rubble, and dying,
dug my way out with a spoon.
I crawled on my elbows when my legs were useless,
dragged loads I couldn't lift, to clear my plot,
nursed a spark from a splintered flint,

and coal, by radiant coal, I have
raised a house of diamonds from the dust.

Kaarina Hollo *Compass*

I'm not diasporic, I'm more
anaphoric, the story begins
and ends on different
lines. Don't categorize
me, I advise you. Your
assumption of origins
is a dead end.

Where does one country start and
the next begin, borders
are orders that I never signed.
History marches through
cities and marshes, the
lines are redrawn and
redrawn again.

So, don't categorize me, I advise you
your assumption of origins is
a dead end
Find the unlined map
The road without signs
The compass in the
blood that knows where and when.

Angela Howarth Marks   *Bungee Jumping Sideways*

Something before memory pushes you out
 and guides as you climb the bars of the cot
  to scramble about knee deep in carpet
   arm deep in cupboards, head deep in chests
    then the door handle drops to your two fingered
   press and the stairs reach up out of sight
    as the garden grows grass from end to end
   with a sand pit, blue ball and woodlice
    under a lavender bush to fall in, a fuchsia bush
     to hide in and a gate to open onto the road
    with a dog to walk and fields to explore
     for blackberries, cowslips, beechnuts and gold
      bikes to ride down to the sea, shrimp pools
     wet towels, seaweed, tide-lines, white horses
      bay horses, lanes that trot out into galloping
     hills, gorse, heather all drumming with hooves
      over ditches, hedges and coloured poles
       into a horse-box to cruise across borders
        to breast growth and books, burning the heart
         but the first wage swirls into make-up and song,
          through doors of night and kisses and clubs
           into lectures and concerts, mail boats and trains
          to exams for tickets to Paris and Rome, gate 21,
          gate 13.B, all aboard for Boston, San Diego to
           Perth, via Nihilism, Taoism, Gurus and Sex till
            the landing lights flash as your belly swells
             and you open your eyes two feet from the ground
              wondering which way is up upside down
               what is the bungee tied to anyway where
                and what is that light pulsing behind you
                 shaping your shadow an arm round your waist
                  and why does it still feel like falling

Richard Kemp   *Hide and Seek*

Someone would always be under the stairs,
or in my aunt's room, inside the wardrobe.
The clever ones would simply crush themselves
and stand behind a door.
But I was the cleverest; I still haven't been found.
I can be talked to, made love with even
and stay unknown.

I migrate, though still walking.
I'm listening to you, I'm nodding seriously, but am high
in the dark over hay smelling cattle.
You explain about filling out time sheets,
I'm separating, reforming and nudging clouds;
I'm landing on a pier
deafening people with my wings.

Peadar O'Donoghue   *Poem for Nobody Who Used to Be*

There have only ever been 3 people
I've been curious to meet:
Gershwin, Anna Karenina, and you.
You may find that surprising?
George died in 1937, fifty one years before I was born and
Anna belongs only in Leon's head;
or on the shelf.
What kind of existence is that? What kind of spark?
Now there's only you and I hope we never meet
but if inevitably we do, it doesn't matter.

It doesn't matter if I am disappointed,
It doesn't matter if we have nothing to say,
It doesn't matter if an awkward chasm of embarrassment
opens up and swallows us if my hand were to brush yours.

It doesn't mean a thing
if you stifle yawns and check the clock one time too many,
or we do our best to hide mutual and instant indifference,
I don't care if we pull up a chair and have a drink but
remain well-meaning strangers on different trains
in opposite directions. It doesn't matter a jot.

What really matters is that I already know you,
have glimpsed you, found you, felt you,
in your words, in your poems, and in my dreams.

Fred Voss   *The Line No One Crosses*

It may be a comb
a man flourishes and waves above his head and then runs
through his hair
to give it that perfect wave before he clocks out
after another 10 hours on the machine
or
a pair of snakeskin boots the black
man at the steel-part-cleaning tub of solvent
wears
and keeps spotlessly clean all day amid the grease
and grime of the factory,
the picture
of a dead wife on the inside of a toolbox lid
or the punch
through the air of a hand that once won a Golden Gloves
championship,
the warble
in a machine shop bathroom stall of a voice that once recorded a record
in Nashville
or the patch
of some long-defunct 60s outlaw motorcycle club
on the sleeveless Levi jacket
of an old man on a drill press,
but whatever it is
machinists stand back
in dread respect and without one trace of laughter leave it well enough
alone,
knowing
that even men
barely getting by on $10-an-hour on oily stinking machines
must have something sacred
they will fight to the death
for.

K. V. Skene   *One Per Person*

We are who we are
the day we are born, we live
at the appropriate distance

in a stone-faced town
where kids collect in corners
like sheep

and houses hold together
long enough
for closets to fill with familial bones

and dissidents rumble down alleyways
brushing up our fears
until we ID

our dear departing – the high-heeled girl
clattering by
every Friday night, the drunk,

tearing at his thin shirt,
as he bleeds
into the street. We don't plan this –

it just happens. The death rate remains
one per person
and everyone wants to believe

they'll be missed. Other people's lives
are never as real
as we want them to be. Tonight,

lying by your side, I confess
I made you up. Trust me.
No one will notice.

Lizann Gorman   *Easily Broken*

He is glass,
see through,
has a label
I cannot read
filled with things
I cannot see.

He is restrained
with a screw
top lid, some
days he feels
too small to
hold his contents.

Áine Herlihy   *Tall Ship Tales*

When the news came in
He granted himself permission to close down.
He found it hard to think in thoughts.
We are a broken people,
We ache in ways we cannot feel.

Paul Birtill   *Near Life Experience*

I stopped keeping a diary
it was getting embarrassing
I had nothing to write about
and somebody might have found it.

Richard Halperin   *The Good Man Asleep in His Chair*

for Paul

There is a certain trust in sleep.
The asleep are so defenceless, with their mouths open
                                    and their necks back,
Their hands slack, holding neither weapons nor flowers.

The only thing that holds him, then – breathing or God.
Though his living room is his, it is not his now.
Though his chair is his chair, he has no hold over it.
He has loosed the cords, his wife and children out somewhere,
His wristwatch unwatched, his hairy legs stretched into the carpet.
He owns nothing now, yet sleeps as if he owns everything.
And, as he is a good man, he does.

Robert Nye   *Drinking Hot Chocolate in the Rain*

Drinking some hot dark chocolate through a hole
In a cardboard cup as the bright rain came down
I saw the market and the people in it
Glorified and transfigured utterly
As if they were the very dream of God.

The chocolate in my cup held some vanilla,
A little stick, a pod I licked just once
As I stood staring at that shining scene,
Knowing that I was in it but not of it.
My tongue went out to taste the raindrops then.

There in the market by that coffee-stall
I saw the world turned inside-out. The rain
Flew upwards like so many crystal sparks
Returning to the glory of the sun
As I drank my dark chocolate to the dregs.

This, this is ecstasy, to stand and drink
Hot chocolate in the rain, lost in a crowd
Of strangers, and to feel for them such love
As Dante felt for Beatrice when he saw
Her passing by and his own heart bowed down.

Ciarán O'Rourke   *Thanksgiving*

for Elizabeth

You bow your chin
So that your eyes
Rest somewhere else,
Far from ours,
From all of this,

Remote momentarily
From the havoc of
Laughter tumbling
Still in the water jug.

I notice how carefully
Each place has been set,

The cutlery clean, the
Perfectly positioned
Butter dish, the napkins
Rolled around themselves
And folded, the bowl of
Crushed cranberries blushing
At the heart of the table,

As the prayer
Of thanks is spoken.

Your smile is touched
By silence now:

More, I know,
Than bread is broken.

Colm Breathnach   *An Iacha*

Bhíodar ag crústach cloch le lacha is a hál ar an gcanáil
nuair a thána orthu, triúr ógánach ar lá faoin dtor.
Ba leor an bhéic a ligeas leo lena gcur á thabhairt dos na bonnaibh
trasna na páirce agus amach thar an bhfalla thall, is leanadar orthu ansan fiú
as radharc ar fad siar an bóthar thar n-ais i dtreo na hóige soineanta
a d'fhágadar ina ndeabhaidh an mhaidin sin ba chosúil.

Ni róbhuíoch a bhíos don lacha chéanna,
a chuir an cathú ar mo thriúr,
mar fiú má ligeadarsan an eachtra i ndearúd ó shin
ní féidir liomsa gan cuimhneamh orm fhéin feasta
ach mar chancrán a ligeann béic cois canálach
ar ógánaigh ar lá múitseála.

Colm Breathnach   *The Duck*

They were pelting stones at a duck and her brood on the canal
when I came upon them, three youths mitching school.
My shout was enough to have them scamper
across the field, out over the wall and onwards
until well out of sight on the road back
towards an innocent childhood left behind that morning, I suppose.

I wasn't too happy with the duck
that had tempted my three buckos
for even if they have since forgotten the incident
I can't help but see myself from now on
as a cantankerous crank shouting by the canal
at these youths on the lang.*

* Cork city slang for truanting
Translated by Gabriel Rosenstock

Liam Ó Muirthile   *Cad É*

Táim ó sheomra go seomra
ar fud an tí
ag lorg rud éigin,
is nach mbeidh fhios agam
cad é nó
go bhfaighidh mé é.

Ní hé an stán aráin é
an plúr garbh donn
ná an plúr mín bán,
cé go dtógaim amach iad
is go gcuirim sa mheá iad
is go ndeinim builín amháin.

Ní haon leabhar a bhíos a léamh é
más buan mo chuimhne
is a leagas uaim,
cé go seasaim ag na seilfeanna
is go bhféachaim tríothu
is go dtéim ar mo ghlúine ar an urlár.

Ní haon eochair a bhí uaim í
ní rabhas ag dul amach
níor fhágas éinní ar siúl,
cé go bhfuilim ó sheomra go seomra
ar fud an tí
ag lorg rud éigin
is nach faic é
is go bhfuiulim ag déanamh bróin chiúin.

Liam Ó Muirthile   *What It Is*

I go from room to room
around the house
looking for something,
and, to be honest, I won't know
what it is
till I find it.

It's not the bread tin,
nor the coarse brown flour,
nor the fine white flour,
though I take them out
and measure them on the scales
and bake a single loaf.

It's not any book I was devouring,
if memory serves me correctly,
which I put down absentmindedly,
although I stand at the shelves
and scan the book stacks
and fall to my knees.

It's not any missing key.
I wasn't going out.
I didn't leave anything on, although
I'm shuffling from room to room
combing the whole house for something
and it's nothing
quietly mourning.

Translated from the Irish by Greg Delanty

Christine Broe   *In the Palm of His Hand?*
                      (Isaiah 49.15)

A part of me is dead, can feel no pain,
the part that feared has nothing left to fear,
now you who gave me birth forget my name.

A stranger now, my visits you disdain.
I come, I see you, and I leave you here
and part of me is dead, can feel no pain.

I try to jog your memory in vain
hand you photographs of those you once held dear,
but you who gave me birth forget my name.

Demolished, derelict your memory lane.
I miss your wicket wit, your Dublin sneer.
Part of me is dead and can feel no pain.

Just a shell of a woman you became,
empty of us oblivious of years.
You gave us birth and now forget our names.

Nameless we come, while breath in you remains.
We'll not forget you, though bereft of tears.
For part of us is dead, can feel no pain
now you who gave us birth forget our names.

Knute Skinner   *She's Back*

'She's back again?'

'She is,' he answered, crossing to the locker
and rummaging for his boots.

'Is she back long then?'

'She is not,' he said, sitting down on the kindling box.
'She showed up last night.'
He forced the stiff cold boots over swollen feet.

'Is she staying long?'

He walked to the door and looked outside
where clouds separated and merged
in a patchy sky.
The cattle yard was trodden mud, all over and back.
'She says not,' he said, and he buttoned up his anorak
and stepped through the doorway.

'She'll be gone soon then?'

He turned on the gravel and looked back
to where I stood, half slumped on the threshold.
I stood there shuddering in the sharp wind
and feeling that wind through my thin bones.
He coughed a minute and he spat
on the wet gravel.
'I don't know,' he replied
and then cleared his throat.

'She's back again then,' I said.

He swung round, facing the wind, and half ran
the long path to the van.

Gabrielle Alioth   *Small Things*

I step from word to word
Over the dark river
And they say the cold will numb me
Before the water pulls me down.

There isn't a shore to reach for
On the half-empty sheet
And they say life will go on
And you haven't even left me.

I saw all those small things
When you loved me
And they say I will see them again
As death is invisible, too.

Michael McCarthy   *Olive*

Often, the sheets are storm-tossed.
Angled elbows, knees, protrude at random. Sometimes
A turbulence of limbs breaks through the surface.
Once, her chest exposed, a withered nipple
Suggested I should look away.

Her spirit is a ship long sunk. Never a hint
Of recognition. I come here to pray with her.
Searching downward – in the blind chance
A prayer might reach her – I stand helpless.
Olive, you are no advert for old age.

Today, a nurse has been to tidy up
The bedclothes smooth and restful.
A radio plays in the background
Rod Stewart, raucous yet melodic:
Have I told you lately that I love you.

Albert Conneely   *The Wink*

For J.P. and M.

After the cutters had gone through him
like a Saxon plough up his chest, after the clamps
and the splitters, and exposed beating heart,
the stents and the stitches, after all that
beneath a pile of tubes and bleeps and noises

She stood watching him, nothing like
the husband took for granted, the let pass
of habit now as if a god had put in a hand
and stirred things up, as if struck
by lightning and laid where he lay, recovering,

Not waking, she calls to him in his far off,
down to him in his deep sea of anaesthesia
where he hears and turns and begins to swim
painfully up, slows in the silence, unsure,
but her calls again are luminescence in the dark

And every unanswered call is an empty hook
in her heart as it beats and she breathes unassisted,
she calls and her calls ring across the stillness
of worry, the fathoms beneath the surface
he approaches, back into the trauma of his body,

And where he breaks one eye open and slowly
winks, he squeezes her hand and sinks
back down to never remember having surfaced
and seen what reaches him in the depths,
and she, easily forgetting, that he ever even

Hears her there.

Mary Woodward   *The Midnight Returns*

A whole city burning to the ground
out there. When last she looked,
pulling back a fraction of the blackout
in the Izal scrubbed patients' bathroom,

it was blazing everywhere. Shoreditch,
Whitechapel, Aldgate. Streaming searchlights;
anti-aircraft guns booming from Hackney Marshes;
the sergeants' voices yelling Fire in her mind.

The ward is silent. Too sick for the shelters
these sleep out the raid, or pretend to,
each bed a curtained cave of safe darkness
in the night lamps' gentian shadow.

She begins the midnight returns,
white cuff moving across the ward ledger,
accounting for each still, breathing body,
initials the careful list, dates it.

There'd be none of this back home, drowsy cows
warm in the shed, hooves smelling of Sligo earth.
She closes the book, glances at the time.
All medication done, each temperature checked.

Fire engines, now, screaming close by.
She prays, of course, mother of god, protect us,
Touching the little ripple of her rosary
in the pocket of her navy dress;

knows nothing promises them another minute;
every circle of her watch hand a victory,
willing their journey to the morning,
to the shrapnel covered pavements, singed pigeons,

the early buses starting up the day.

DYING

Bruce James   *Tenderly*

Meditation on dying of cancer

Some tears
Are like the hunger
Amongst dying people

Some hunger
Is like the tears amongst dying people

Some prayers
Are like the kisses amongst dying people

Some kisses
Are like the prayers
Amongst dying people

Some tears
Are like prayers

St Valentine's Day 2011
Bruce died on March 9th, 2011

Medbh McGuckian   *Angelica Flowerhead from Underneath*

Dramatic horseshoe of beeches, whose leaves
Have simply unwrapped to a fluffy garden.
Why do you feel you have been there in the past?

The house is shaking itself gently, for no reason,
And I am weary of its modulations, delicate
Though they be, like a tree slowly melting,
Or a maternal hand over the hair,
Inhaling your silken back.

One should listen as it were, against them,
Some of life's ingredients, the horseshoe
That dented somebody's head, so that
Her blood poured out for his bath and her veins
Were woven into a little dress for him.

The treatment last winter could not check it.
Nothing can check it now, since clouds
Have inscrutable wills to swell across
The wind-thrown milky sunshine where
A lost golf ball is caught in a chaplet of bluebells.

Not till I have crossed another border
Will a life arrive, though inside that grey
No heart can yet flow. Mostly untouched,
She watches the longing with which her friend
Kisses the spotlighted earring, the heaven
A star is to the floor of time,

The petals bursting to the rosary,
Feast-day opening of a winged altar.

Colin Graham   *Sika*

When you hear the shriek of a Sika deer,
Seeing you first on your night-time field walk,
Calm yourself, swing the beam through the trees,
Lift the wood pigeons out of their roosts,
And call to mind the example of one
Who sheltered a fawn in his tractor cab
Admiring its dapple and twigs-for-legs,
And a week later, his lines of berries
Strafed by the herd – flicking white tails
Out of tempo with the country music
Playing in the darkness to scare them off –
Found a stag caught, blood daubing barbed wire,
Looked into its eye, stroked its shifting spine,
And choked it with hands muddy from planting.

Hammond Journeaux

98

Paula Meehan   *The Last Thing*

        my ebbing father said to me was
not the wind before he slipped below
the horizon of his morphine dream.

So was it the moon in the hospice
rigging? Or the cloud's buoyant shadow?
Or my mother's voice helming him home?

No. I think it was some ferocious
winged creature at the ward's window
breast feathers flecked with salt laced foam.

DEATH

Marguerite Colgar *Bridgie, Keeper of the Fire*

She rolled on worn hips, carried in
hard black sods, wind-dry bog dale
her fire burned bright for welcome callers
butter drooled on hot potato cakes
greying ash signalled a visit's end.

Sunset was her time, she watched
high summer flame blacken
the Scotch House at Ogull,
then slow retreat to a ball of fire
sliding seaward at the Bill's Rock.

Born in sight and sound of wave,
she left school early
learned life in Scotland drudgery
married and brought him home
nurtured her clutch.

I sit at her kitchen windowsill
Set again her fat dictionary, magnifying
glass, crosswords and *Ireland's Own*,
recall her quick wit,
her telling and her listening,
light touch on history, *sure the past is gone.*

Burn everything when I die
keep nothing, not even a shoe
life is to go on, no keening
no standing at the grave like geidimeens.

geidimeen: an annoying flighty person

Jo Pestel   *Past the Post*

Wouldn't you know, she said
wouldn't you know he'd do
something like this, upping and
dying on me the minute
we'd got things to rights,
everything paid off, able at last
to sit down beholden to no-one?
Too early all his life long
rushing us out of the house
at half past nine
for a ten o'clock kick-off;
up at the bar getting the first round
before you knew
what you wanted, top of the queue
on parents' evenings – as though that
would make any difference –
and to my dying day
I'll remember the garden
with that ton of coal cheap in June
and the children filthy all summer.
Oh yes, flashing his camera
for the angle at christenings, the signing
at weddings, bantam-cock pleased
crowing over the rest of them,
leaving me chasing the back of him these
twenty-five years, juggling Peter and Paul.
Well, who's laughing now? That's
what I'd like to know. Not him
from that dead surprised look on his face
with all heaven probably
caught on the hop, and sweetest Jesus
how will I face the days and the nights
without him pestering?

Seán Ó Tuama   *Nuair Shínfead Siar*

A Chríost ná scaoil orm an bás i gan fhios
Mar scaoilis orm codhladh inné,
Ach deonaigh dom an mhíogarnach ghnáthúil
Sara gcartfaidh siad an teampall cré . . .

Chun ná dúiseoinn, 's gur díthreabh mo dhúchas,
Tir nárbh col dom bean ná gaol,
Sceach-bhall ceoigh 'nar shearg na finniúna
Mhilseodh an teanga, reamhar le scéan.

Go n-atfadh romham go sleamhain insa chiúineas
An abhainn dhubh le múnlach daol,
Go labharfadh chugam an eala le muc-ghnúsacht
'S an gadhar bacach le tíogar-bhéic.

Gurbh iad na héin a cheolfadh dom gan suaimhneas,
Ceirteacha uaigneacha le gaoth
Ag liobar-chaint 's ag seint go stracaithe
Ar shreanga teileafóin an aeir.

Go bhfliuchfaí mé sa cheo, is fós ná silfeadh
Aon bhraon le fuarthan ar mo bhéal,
Go siúlfainn is go siúlfainn i measc daoine
Ag prap-ghluaiseacht mar bhréagáin ar théid . . .

A Chríost ná scaoil orm mo chodladh i gan fhios
Mar scaoilis orm bás inné,
Ach deonaigh dom cnead-mhíogarnach ghnáthúil
An tseanduine i ndeireadh an lae.
Chun go leagfad fén gcathaoir mo léine chaite,
Oíche shailm-chiúin, tráth Tenebrae,
Is go bhfáiscfead fém chulaith suain mo chrios, le teannas,
'S go sínfead siar mo theampall cré.

Seán Ó Tuama   *When I Lay Back*

Oh Christ don't send death unawares
like yesterday's sleep.
Grant me rest before
I cast this clay away.

    Don't let me wake to wilderness,
    a land of the unknown
    where vines wither in mist,
    are sweet on my terrified tongue.

    Where the putrid stream
    swells slyly in silence;
    where the swans grunt like swine
    and the lame dog roars.

    Where birds sing incessantly
    like lonely rags, windblown,
    blubbering, babbling a broken
    Morse to telegraph wires.

    Where mist would soak me,
    yet leave me thirsty,
    where I'd wander among throngs
    awkward as a marionette.

Oh Christ don't send sleep unawares
as you loosed death yesterday
but permit a fitful sleep
to a tired old man
and I will put away my old shirt
under the seat at Tenebrae
and psalm peaceful I'll buckle
tight my belt beneath my shift
and put aside this clay.

Translated from the Irish by Nigel McLoughlin

Eamon Grennan — *Obit*

27.2.00, i.m. Adele Dalsimer

The hare that takes its time crossing the drowned garden
And stopping to nibble little bits of what takes its fancy
Doesn't know the bad news I've gathered from the newspaper
I was carefully crumpling for the fire this stormy morning
And neither does the clackering magpie nor tikketting wren

And the wind that shakes by the scruff the flayed branches
Hasn't heard a word of it though it stops me cold and
On my knees like this staring down at the calm light
Of her face and the mischievous amusement in her eyes
Shining up at me among the other names of the freshly dead.

Mary Norman

Bernard O'Donoghue   *Dockets*

'and this, your all-licens'd fool'

Although it's hard to think what he would buy
requiring a receipt – his needs being met
by the cluster of silver and copper pushed
along the counter for the next pint and half-one –
when he was found a few days dead in the house
he'd squatted in with dogs for thirty years,
there was a neat pile of dockets from the creamery store
held in place by the red inner stone
of a pre-electric iron. Proof of what?
That his life was ordered in its way:
exactly how much to drink, in what proportions,
to go home happy, and yet able to get up
and stalk past curious windows, eyes ahead,
and spend the day painting from a ladder?

Could he have been Jimmy the Householder?
Or Jimmy the Clerk, who might in a different life
have been the man in red tie and tweed jacket
who carried the neat brown attaché case
to the Stations for the priest, and snapped
its fasteners open on the trestled kitchen table,
shouldered by two chairs, disguised for Mass
beneath the candles and starched white linen cloth,
to reveal the vessels of the Sacrament:
ciborium, amice, maniple and stole?

Oliver Bernard   *XVI*

from XLVII Poems

the wonder of landscape is to the wonder of people
as two plus one is to the square root of minus nothing
by which I mean that if you are very careful indeed
you can do the sum but to begin to get a grasp of the
concept
you have to have help and I know that I am the man
who was beginning to be cured of his blindness and
cried out
I see men as trees walking and was filled with the wonder
of it

except that I am not at all sure that I shall be cured
in my case there seem to be hints of a possible relapse
if I don't go on looking if I don't go on trying to see
it will all go away again and my eyes only express salt water

sometimes it seems to help to get it all down on paper
as if registering and recording the occasional remission
gave you something to hold on to but it is just pieces of
paper
you are holding is it or can you read again what you have
written
and feel again as sure as you felt when you wrote it
or can you leave these pieces of paper on the table in the
room upstairs
with your corpse on the bed with its shoulders turned to
the wall
and think they will be found and not lit to see
whether
you really are dead yes I'm sorry but this time you are

Anthony Keating   *In a Professional Capacity*

She handed me a piece of paper,
Patterned with the cipher
Of a curiously rational hand:

'Night has become too dark,
For me to swim to shore,
My life belongs to history,
My memory to you.'

And asked:

'What was he thinking?
Was there anything I could have done?'

Mounting platitudes,
I identified the usual suspects,
Wishing I had more to offer her,
I longed for his economy.

Floyd Skloot   *Latin Lessons*

The daughter of the local florist taught
us Latin in the seventh grade. We sat
like hothouse flowers nodding in a mist
of conjugations, declining nouns that
made little sense and adjectives that missed
the point. She was elegant, shapely, taut.
She was dazzling and classic, a perfect
example to us of such absolute
adjectives as *quite* or *too* or *perfect*.
The room held light. Suffering from acute
puberty, we could still learn case by case
to translate with her from the ancient tongue
by looking past her body to the chaste
scribblings she left on the board. We were young
but knew that the ablative absolute
was not the last word in being a part
of something while feeling ourselves apart
from everything that mattered most. We chased
each other on the ballfield after class
though it did no good. What we caught was not
what we were after, no matter how fast
we ran. She first got sick in early fall.
A change in her voice, a flicker of pain
across her face, and nothing was the same.
She came back to us pale and more slender
than ever, a phantom orchid in strong
wind, correcting our pronoun and gender
agreement, verb tense, going over all
we had forgotten while she was gone. Long
before she left for good in early spring,
she made sure the dead language would remain
alive inside us like a buried spring.

Chuck Kruger   *The Tao of Non-Physics*

In the high middle of stony nowhere a single
bubble rises through the altar of crusty earth
up into a pool, quiet, brimming, and as he watched,
up welled another, another, pure as the flap
of butterfly wing-creation that doesn't, as chaos
theory cries, touch hearts at first and later
crumble cities – and he wondered where it will end
if end it does, or can, and when. In next
autumn's gale? He stooped, cupped hands, from finger
bowl sipped. The coolness of the water soothed
his thoughts. He watched overflow, trickle after trickle,
go as slow, as shyly, as woodland wren
hops into hole away from home for that
initial prowl. He followed after flow,
and in mere miles a tumbling torrent
raged brown through forest, poured over edge,
cascaded into gully, and he walked with
giant steps beside a river growing wider, wilder,
rapids, primary pools where heron ruled,
houses, boats, a bridge, and he saw
river empty into sea, flushed out, finished,
and then a thought bubbled up, trickled
into mainstream mind: he considered the way
that death makes life worthwhile: take away
the sea, the end, and then there's no beginning.
He considered the way that muddy water comes
from purity and to purity goes. As much miracle
as wren, as spring, as butterfly wing, as sea,
is good old consciousness, what makes life
worth dying for, what too can trickle,
burst its banks, trip over cliffs, and always
empty somewhere into sea. If he'd
no end, there'd be no dying then and he,
why he'd not even bother contemplate the meekest
trickle through the altar of this crusty earth.

James Aitchison   *On the Way to the River*

I was too young to listen with intent
to the river singing on its shingle bed.
I didn't hear the song implant its sound
but I knew its music when I went back again.

On the way to the river
my prickling scalp and the earth's unsteadiness
proved the nearness of the beast
watching me from a cave among the rocks.
I was aged seven or eight:
I knew the beast was unsayable;
I knew I was too old to hold your hand.

You said, 'Wild garlic.' You said, 'Marsh marigolds.'
And when you said, 'These are hazel trees,'
the thicket and the name eclipsed the sun.

My nameless beast,
your naming of flowers and trees
and the river making music visible
gave my boyhood a pagan holiness.

My mind was smaller than my feral brain.

You were too ill to say, 'Goodbye.'
On clouded, moonless, starless nights I wept
and in the dark I reached out for your hand.

Gerry Boland   *Drowning*

Drowning off a safe beach is not difficult.
Atlantic waves, a retreating tide, a sharp
belt of a body board, and lifeguards
swimming to a false alarm a lifetime away.

It's all over in minutes, though
it hasn't yet begun for your mother,
who is happy you are happy, here
on this warm August afternoon.

She looks up from her book,
smiles expectantly, scans the sand
for her only child, sees a gathering
commotion at the water's edge

out of the corner of her eye.

Frank Farrelly   *Birdwatcher*

He comes late to class, avoids the crush,
sits still, wordless. You observe his comings,
his goings, ensure he makes it through unscathed.
His eyes speak trust, make you feel responsible.
Others never worry you much
– flock together safe in packs, mouth off at ease.

You imagine him in the loud yard, attuned to
cries from seagulls overhead, or on the cliff
on weekend afternoons to spy a kittiwake,
sketch its grey wing, legs of inky-black.

Remember his pictures on your desk, proudly spread;
an oystercatcher's bill, a riding eagle's golden mane,
how much it meant to you, to him.

Then one night the tide creeps up and drowns him
where he sleeps below the dunes where redshanks
tread in secret pools.

Nothing prepares you for this. Not tragedies you teach;
the girl who begs her lover's blade to rust her heart,
the boy whose brother killed his hawk
Bloodless words on bloodless sheets.

Afric McGlinchey   *The Seekers*

(i.m. Andrew)

Now they are tracking the cliffs,
Men at the drop, women further in
scattered widely, but bound by the silken cord
of him

There is his brother, deranged and staggering, alone
No-one dares go near, for fear of edges
A tiny cove, some tracks, shoes and clothes neatly stacked

The divers move east and west, into the depths, crevices
beaches are combed
Some walk with sticks, and in pairs,
murmuring

The air, chill and unmoving, ghostlike against our faces
sweep of dune grasses, crunch of footsteps, a few words
launched on the breeze

Some hours, days, pass and there is a gathering at the beach,
where the father speaks, gently, grateful
the weight of emotion, too dense to lift alone

Not like the weight, finally found,
unbound now, floating, free

Arlene Ang   *The Day She Was Called to Identify the Body*

The windows crystallised late August:
still life with calendar, *Architectural Digest*.
The house wore heat like hosiery.
She took out a pack of tofu from the paper bag.
A gold pendant drummed against
her breastbone as tomatoes sliced themselves
from her hands. She thought in terms
of neon signs – the bars, the motel rooms,
the shops, the theatres that rolled
down streets like empty beer bottles.
The police grew in her hair
and reeked of runaway afternoon.
She said she didn't know who they wanted her
to think it was. She said, like that time
at the bus stop when he said he never wanted
to see her again, *This isn't my son*.
She gave them his age:
thirteen years, seven months and six days.
She stopped remembering anything else.

Ann Gray   *Your Body*

I identified your face
and when he said is this, and gave your full name,
it wasn't enough to say, yes, he said I had to say,
this is, and give your full name.
It seemed to be all about names, but I only saw your face.
I wanted to rip back the sheet and say, yes this is his chest,
his belly, these are his balls and this the curve of his buttock.
I could have identified your feet, the moons on your nails,
the perfect squash ball of a bruise on your back,
the soft curl of your penis when it sleeps against your thigh.
I wanted to lay my head against your chest, to take your hands,
hold them to my face, but I was afraid your broken arm was hurting.
My fingers fumbled at your shirt but the makeshift sling had trapped it.
Your shirt, your crisp white shirt. The shirt I'd ironed on Friday.
The shirt that grazed my face when you leaned across our bed
to say goodbye. I watched the place where your neck
joins the power of your chest and thought about my head there.
He offered me your clothes. I refused to take your clothes.
Days later I wanted all your clothes. I didn't know what I wanted,
standing there beside you, asking if I could touch you,
my hands on your cheek. He offered me a lock of your hair.
I took the scissors. I had my fingers in your hair.
I could taste the black silken hair of your sex.
I wanted to wail all the Songs of Solomon,
I wanted to throw myself the length of you and wail.
I wanted to lay my face against your cheek.
I wanted to take the blood from your temple with my tongue,
I wanted to stay beside you till you woke.
I wanted to gather you up in some impossible way
to take you from this white and sterile place to somewhere
where we could lie and talk of love.
I wanted to tear off my clothes, hold myself against you.
He said, *take as long as you want*, but he watched me
through a window and everything I wanted seemed
undignified and hopeless, so I told him we could go,
we could leave, and I left you
lying on the narrow bed, your arm tied in its sling,
purple deepening the sockets of your eyes.

A. M. Cousins   *Tarmac*

For Garda Adrian Donohoe
(1971-2013)

When Death was a sacrament and needed to lie down,
preferably on a feather bed with cool white sheets
          and a quilt made from the remnants
of your great-aunts' tea-dresses,
there was a candle,
blessed and holy,
steadied in your hand by a neighbour's;
sacred oils and Extreme Unction;
a litany of saints and martyrs to light, to guard, to guide you;
and tears on a face of love.

So.
When smoke and badness billowed from the car-window;
when the shotgun's snout slid out and answered
          the policeman's knock,
who was your face of love?

Tell me that the old ones climbed the stile,
or slipped through the bars of the gate,
rustled their way up the hill and along the road
in their sepia gowns and wedding-suits,
that they knelt on the wet tarmac and cradled your head
          and held your hand.
Tell me that they looked on your face with love.

Rory Johnston   *The Pension Book*

Out of sight, around the first corner
He vomited their hospitality
Into their neighbour's field.

The Excise man called to deliver
The pension book, March 1933
In the wild cold of Donegal.

A wee gaunt woman at the half-door
Welcomed the gauger. Not everyone in that
Pauper poteen parish held such a welcome.

The old man slept, slumped in his chair in
Front of an empty grate, amid the smell of
Incontinence and yesterday's boiled cabbage.

The visitor drank black tea without sugar
From a cracked dirty cup with no handle
The old lady drank from a battered tin mug.

When the boys come home from Scotland after
The potato picking, there'll be a few pounds,
And maybe a letter from America soon.

She shuffled to the sleeping man and tucked the
Dirty coat around him. *Sure let the poor divil*
Sleep, won't my X do as good.

A trembling hand marked her simple X.
The bilious gauger left, his stomach churning,
And wondered how long the old man was dead.

Paddy Bushe   *Ritual for the Propitiation of the Abnormal Dead*

Among the Naxi, the Dongba priests,
With flags and images, grain and eggs,
Build a Village of the Abnormal Dead
Where the wandering spirits of those who died
By murder, suicide and war are danced
Into quietude, their village gently destroyed.

I would have them dance all over Ireland,
In towns and villages, and along ditches
Where bodies have been found, and not found.
I would have them dance in Greysteel and in Omagh,
In Monaghan, Soloheadbeg and Kilmainham.
I would have them dance in Enniskillen, Béal na Bláth,
In Ravensdale and Ballyseedy, Talbot Street and Warrenpoint.

I would have them dance every bloody sunday
And weekday until only the everyday
Spirits are abroad for their allotted time,
Before they rest, and let the living live.

FUNERALS

Michael O'Dea   *Katy Tyrrell's Wake*

1
When Katy Tyrrell's eyelids were closed,
they stopped the clock,
covered the mirror,
 and she was waked.

Entwined in her hands, a rosary beads,
'Je suis L'imaculée conception'
was embroidered on her shroud;

everyone said she looked every inch a Cherokee.

2
After she was laid out, and the ticking stopped
and a sheet blocking the devil's door,

he said, 'Let's sit down to a game.
Shuffle the cards, dale herself in.'

'Layve the window open
and mind, don't step in her way.'

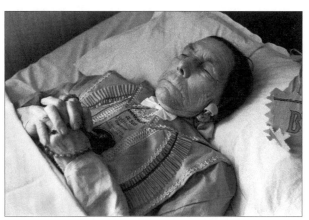

John Minihan

119

Peggie Gallagher   *The Magician*

You're here again.
With a flick of the wrist
you throw the switch on your own wake.

The dresser dense and pitted with age.
Candles flickering against the window nets.
The polished coffin on its make-shift trestle.

Same scatter of neighbours and long-
dead relatives, their susurrus of prayers.
Here's the part you like best:

The way the grandchildren clamour in
trailing the guttery muck from the cow's drain –
hard to tell fear from excitement on their clear
                                    morning faces.
What is it? you ask. The air stills.
Three sets of wellies move to the box.

They're anxious to tell you, bring you the news,
spilling out words like shining coins – the cow, the calf,
the shimmering, slithering river, the red-stained veil,
the heft and bellow of birth, its livid chrism.
The silk-sleeved calf staggering to its feet.
And Granddad, she licked him and licked him and licked him.

Marie Dullaghan   *When You Are Dead*

I will not bury you in cold clay, your bones waiting
while your flesh decays, worms in your hair and mud
rotting your eyes. I will not bury you in the damp earth.

I would rather send you to the fire, and weep
while you dance and play with the flames;
grieve, while your smoke caresses the tree tops.

I will gather your ash in a clay pot or in wood
and spill its greyness into the fastest river;
mourn while you travel on, down waterfalls

and through bright meadows, until at last
you arrive at the unending ocean, its unceasing
motion like a baby's cradle or an old man's

rocking chair. And there, my lovely, you may have
charge of all the wild forces of that open space –
the explosion of sun, the cold of the moon,

the exhilaration of unbridled storms – lightning,
thunder, roaring wind and soaring wave –
you, the maestro conducting his orchestra.

Richard Toovey   *The Body Only*

in memoriam JPD

And if it is the body only
which has brought us back to take our leave,
well, it is worthy of the ceremony,
having served and made the man we love
now that we see his body lying lonely
in the clothes he wore when still alive,
separate from sense and memory
and all we gradually gave.

Still we stand before a mystery
and do not know for what we grieve,
what we walk with to the grave,
who we find there, who we leave,
except that it is in ourselves
and that we share it, silently.

Mary O'Malley   *After the Funeral, the Departure*

The bags are badly packed, is a last look allowed?
Before I leave I'll dust the lovely perfume flasks and wrap them
In a silk scarf like metaphors or torahs, storm green, chalice red
And a gold flecked cobalt I bought in Israel.

They have survived the rock splitting under the house,
The walls straining like weightlifters' arms, the noise.
I have seen objects as delicate in a New York museum,
A pretty Etruscan amphora beside some Spartan vases.

Time to roll up my sleeves, there is domestic work
Waiting – knives to be sharpened, the house scoured, a grave
To be dug. Even if I am incompetent and hear the tough
Women laughing at my efforts, see the disgust carved

Into their faces as I sit with my forehead on the foot
Of a sunken grave, let them be disgusted. I am disgusted myself.
I didn't see it boomeranging back to the weak spots until it hit –
The ga bolga in the heart, the eye, the right breast.

All that remains is to let the wind read each face accurately –
To say goodbye lightly would be nice but I do not;
I move on reluctantly, like every daughter of history
Who has left her father's house unwillingly or late.

The ga bolga was the javelin-like weapon used by Cuchulainn.

LOSS AND BEREAVEMENT

Padraig Rooney   *The Tow Horses*

Why have I come down this old towpath
by the disused canal to find the horses
grazing at the far end of the meadow,
under the trees by the Blackwater river?

They approach as though they know me
and begin to nuzzle the paling wire
for sugar cubes my mother fed them,
my mother long dead, the horses too.

Shane Martin   *I Thought I Heard Him*

I thought I heard him in the yard
As the steel coal buckets kissed
His boots munching on the gravel
As the coal lumps were scooped
And slid into rows along the wall.

I thought I heard him in the grasses
Scattering hen-meal, eyeing birds
Him overlooking the roof tiles
Towards the swans on Lisanisk
As his thoughts dashed and dived.

I thought I heard him with paint tins
Stirring new colours out of the old
Striking lines with chalk and cord
On the white plywood boards
Him muttering with the transistor.

I thought I heard him at the gable wall
Letting potato bags slump in line
Dragging sacks of blocks for the fires
That would burn until the nights died
Like memories smouldering in my dreams.

Cathal Ó Searcaigh   *An tEargal*

Agus tú sna blianta deireanacha
cromadh agus liathadh na haoise ag teacht ar do chorp,
ghlac an tEargal seilbh ort.

Spréigh sé a ghéaga beannacha
thart ort go teann. Ar ard a dhroma,
thógadh sé leis chun na spéire tú, uair sa ré.

Líon sé do shúile, do shamhlaíocht,
lena liathacht, lena láidreacht, lena loinne
D'fhág sé d'inchinn i nglas binne.

D'fhás féasóg fraoigh ar leargacha
do leicinn, scraith ar do shúile, crotal liathbhán
ar bhinn do chinn ó bhun go héadan.

Tráthnónta agus an ghrian ag gabháil faoi
luíodh an solas ort go sochmaidh, ag baint gealáin
as grianchloch do ghruaidhe, as eibhear d'éadain.

D'éirigh do bhriathra géar agus spíceach;
clocha scilig a sciorr anuas achan lá le fánaidh
ó mhalaidh crochta do theangaidh.

Diaidh ar ndiadh, chrioslaigh sé tú
lena dhúnáras rúnda , lena dhúchas dúr, lena mhúr draíochta.
D'ordaigh sé leis tú chun na síoraíochta.

Nuair a amharcaim ar an tsliabh anois
stánann tusa orm go síoraí ó gach starrán, ó gach ball.
Tá seilbh glactha agat ar an Eargal.

Cathal Ó Searcaigh   *Errigal*

In your last few years
as your body hunched and greyed with age
Errigal took possession of you.

It spread its angular limbs
tightly around you, shouldering you
every so often high up towards the sky.

It filled your eyes, your imagination
with its muscular, grey bareness.
Your mind was immured in its peak.

A heathery beard clung to the slopes
of your face, a scraw on your eyes, hoary lichen
from the back of your head to your forehead.

In the evenings, at sunset, the light
lay placidly on you, coaxing a gleam
from your quartz cheek, your granite forehead.

Your language grew sharp, became spiked;
a rockfall of scree slid every day
from the steep incline of your tongue.

Slowly but surely, you were crystallized
by its citadel, its gloomy face, its spellbound wall.
It enthralled you towards its eternity.

Now when I look at the mountain
your stare is constant from every overhang and hollow.
You have taken possession of Errigal.

Translated from the Irish by Paddy Bushe

Denise Blake   *Fishing Time*

I always knew this black and white photograph would exist:
three boys standing in a bath-sized boat that is tied pier-side.
They are holding up thin cord lines weighted by hooks like trophies.
You're at the end in wash-faded clothes, all floppy haired and smiling.

What age are you there? Ten? Eleven? By sixteen you were inland
at a counter job. How much did it hurt to move from Schull?
The solid ground scourged your feet, weakened your leg muscles,
and the air, in that northern place, hadn't any sea-salt, only dry dust.

Our instinct led us, on family holidays, climbing into multi-tied boats
to reach the furthest one, any old board, so long as we could travel.
A shoal of silver bellied mackerel sprung from the harbour's waters
as we strained to row farther than the fraying rope would let us go.

For you the rope has always been straining,
all those years when your own boat lay landlocked on our lawn,
all those years when grandchildren leapt into imaginary oceans
until that old boat became so bone dry it would have drowned.

2.

Why do we just travel this far now for the sicknesses and the deaths,
when it is only here that we can stand graveside as soul-pure sails
float towards melting amber; only here will the tides turn from tear-blue
to kingfisher-blue, and here the air brings out the freckles of your youth.

Now while we file away the remnants of your brother's life,
the sea has calmed to heartbeat still. I hear the waves whisper.
Down by barnacled rocks a seal watches with the eyes of Father Time.
I feel all this in my earth-clogged veins, what of your ocean blood?

You can stay indoors and small talk through responsibilities,
but by the morning Fastnet Rock will be far from your back again.
The last of those three boys needs to climb into a pier-side boat.
Go fishing Dad, cast it all away for a light line and a hook-sized weight.

Sheila Killian   *For Yvonne*

Since you died we've been walking
around with no skin.
Up High Street, the coffeeshops,
wind peeling our veins.

People brush against us.
They don't notice
that we have no skin.

All those songs on the radio
some girl with your hair
all blow in, unfiltered

When our new skin grows
we'll be safe again, sheltered
but for now I think we
should stay out of the wind

Jeanette McCullough

Christine James *Disgwyl*

Aber-fan, Hydref 2006

Am ei bod hi eto'n brynhawn
fel pob prynhawn arall, mae'n taenu eto
drwch o fenyn cartre ar ddwy dafell
a gosod y caws yn deidi ger y jam
cyn gwylchu'r te am dri,
a'r fodfedd laeth ar waelod cwpan bach
yn barod iddo fel y bydd bob tro.

Ac am ei bod hi eto'n brynhawn
fel pob prynhawn arall, â eto
at y stepyn i sgwrio'r stryd,
gan gribinio trwy'r wynebau ffres,
y clymau cyfeillion,
am wyrth mewn siwmper wau
yn rhedeg ati eto fel y gwnâi bob tro.

Ac am ei bod hi nawr yn hwyr
a'r tamaid te yn crino ar y plât,
mae'n setlo'i hunan eto wrth y tân,
ei breuddwyd gwrach yn bwysau a rei gweill
a gwyr wrth wylio naid y fflamau gwneud
na fydd 'r un rhwystro arno nawr:
daw ati, bob nos, yn ddi-ffael.

Christine James   *In Expectation*

Aber-fan, October 2006*

As it's afternoon now yet again
like every other afternoon, she yet again
spreads butter thickly on two slices,
sets cheese just so beside the jam
and scalds the tea at three,
an inch of milk poured in a little cup
all ready for him as it always is.

And as it's afternoon now yet again
like every other afternoon, she yet again
goes to the step to scour the street,
combing through fresh faces,
tangled friends,
for a miracle in home-made jumper
running to her as he always would.

And as by now the day is drawing on,
the scrap of tea long curled up on the plate,
she settles, yet again, before the fire,
a weight of wild dreams on her knitting pins;
and knows while watching artificial flame
that nothing now will hinder his return
to her: he comes every night without fail.

** On 21 October 1966, waste from a nearby coal-mine
slid down the hillside and engulfed a primary school
and a number of houses in the village of Aber-fan in
industrial south Wales, killing 116 children and 28 adults.*

Fiona Moore   *1010101010 . . .*

Your death kills me a thousand times.
The tyranny of repetition.

Your death works in binary mode
on/off, forget/remember –
a cold code to decipher,
too late for us.

You/me, here/there.
Zero/one.

Peter Porter   *Deuterothanatos*

I have found a poem in your childish hand
carefully dated 'aged thirteen years, ten months'
which speaks of the 'low golden light'
and of the coming of what, unknown to you
as such, is clearly death. Though we are born
once only, we die several times. If our
single entitled death defines us, something
of it may be shown beforehand. In
the poem you greet the unknown greater world
with a sweet bold welcoming sense, almost
an entreaty. But what confidence remains
that on that lonely morning when you died
your seeming change proved true and that those calm
confiding words had not been overwhelmed
by terror. I see myself revealed
in the dictionary as someone
practising deuterogamy, second-
guessing what's to come, with you ahead,
the light still low and perhaps goldening.

Michelle O'Sullivan   *Letter to U*

Somewhere across time's divide, you are sitting down
with a mug of sweetened tea, its woody scent unfolding
in the steam; heat drowses and warms between your palms.

Sunlight fishes in the eucalyptus, the long line of poplars
that grow shorter in the distance and the heavy rain that fell
last night is mixing silvers in the leafy, narcotic greens.

I wonder what you've scavenged from the silence that sleeps
like a dog at your feet, your ear sharp as a fine-toothed comb;
have you put a hand to the side of your head, like a shell?

On this side of the world, my garden is quiet, still as the stones
that stand in a cemetery. I don't want to envy the resilience of trees
or the flower that grows and glows like an opal in their shade –

                                            but I do.

I have put a hand to my forehead, covered my eyes.
I try hard to imagine that it isn't yours.

Alice Hoult

Ruth O'Callaghan   *Transience*

A stealth of snowfalls, frugal, does not settle
on leaves wet-bright

the way sun after rain
on the playground tarmac dazzles the eyes

of children who witness the seasons passing
the windows of the schoolroom.

It will always be this:
a scripture of sun, a drowse of voices beyond

and, later, a snaggle of rain caught in her hair
the church quiet in candlelight

years of blessings
before grief held close and the snow treacherous

the afternoon white and none to call a name
none to hear a name called

or witness the constancy
of these snowdrops in winter's early darkening.

Sam Burnside   *An Epithalamium*

You are leaving; but, where-
ever you are,
the memories will survive:
so, this memory shall remain –
on your bedpost pegged –
this knobbly, wobbly stocking
fit for some Goblin's fat leg,
misshapen and bulging,
overflowing at the mouth
with goods, all for you –
an apple, the biggest ever conceived,
the most orange-orange ever seen,
twelve wooden bricks,
the brownest and bluest ever imagined:
a sock-full of love:
ah, so light a burden, yet so strong,
made from silken threads,
love-spun, air-carried,
for so long, for so long,
strings from our hearts to your heart to our hearts.

NATURE

Stephen Devereux   *Nothing Else in the Universe Remembers*

Nothing else in the universe remembers.
Only hunger's hunger thinks.
The shrew's sneeze calls to the hawk's sinews,
The sweet stink of grass tells sheep's teeth to gnaw
The river points the salmon to its grave,
Polaris holds the swallow's right eye
So that at dawn
She finds herself where she was born.

Nothing else in the universe forgets.
The ticking of atoms keeps the granite hard.
Gravity maps out the shape of every galaxy,
The maggot tells itself to make a fly.
My cells will know just when to start
The clots in me that stopped my father's heart.

Jeanette McCullough

William Wall   *Singing the Silence*

swifts drill for darkness in a cliff face
the sea eats gravel and spits sand
the limitless fertility of the tide race

who believes in bladder-wrack barnacles
hermit crabs in their hard hats
lined with perfectly symmetrical

mother of pearl turning in spirals
towards an infinitely small
inner space busy with nothingness

the singing silence of the inner ear
and the sea in the sound
the inter-tidal suck in the stones of the pier

the revenant of ancient hurricanes
a million miles distant
human brain-shaped whelk egg-cases

dogfish fin-whales and dolphins
the future is in the rock pools
a single limpet contains the elements

necessary for everything to begin again
never mind if this beginning
ends in a creature that cannot sing

Alwyn Marriage   *Lighter*

Look! he said, flicking his thumb
down over the tiny ratchet wheel.
I did, and as the flame rose up, he held
both cigarette lighter and my attention
in his hand.

Three hundred million years ago, he said,
sunlight absorbed by plants was trapped, dragged
down and buried with them as they died, decayed
in darkness, were compacted holding tight
to sun-squandered energy and light.

Geological gestation through millennia
squeezed plant matter into drip
of liquid gold. Somnolent ooze of oil
lay pregnant with power as human life evolved,
until our need or greed or ingenuity

released sun's ancient energy to serve
new solipsistic purposes. Godlike,
we lit the sunlight, combusted fossil fuels:
methane, ethane, propane, butane,
sunshine re-born in power.

Mesmerised by the unimaginably long time-span
and the tiny flickering flame in the darkening room,
my mind turned inside out. *We squander it*, he said.
We cannot replenish the supply, will leave
no reserves to warm or light those born too late.

Like this.... He blew
the flame out, carefully released the catch
and, lighter poised, flint still, stretched out
the silence as our eyes became
accustomed to the gloom.

Michael Hartnett   *Sinsir*

Dobharchú mé, biolar mo bhrat
brácaim an bradán, mo bhráthair.
Breac mé is eascann faoi bhun easa,
saighead uisce is lúbaire –
breac mé is bradán,
dobharchú, eascann.
Mise an spéir, an t-aer is an tEarrach
mise an t-iasc is an t-uisce
mise an chré faoi mo chosa
Dia agus duine
réalta mise i measc na n-ardreann
mise na hardreanna, de shoilse déanta
mise an t-éan is an t-ainmhí
clúmh agus fionnadh
ainmhí éanúil aonarach aonta mise
eolas ag borradh i mo chloigeann
mar shíolbhach i mblaosc uibhe
anam is intinn is intleacht bric
anam is intinn is intleacht toir
anam is intinn is intleacht fir
duine agus cruinne.

Hammond Journeaux

140

Michael Hartnett   *Ancestors*

I am an otter, the watercress my mantle,
    hook of the salmon, my brother.
I am a trout, an eel coiling under
    the shaft of a waterfall.
Arrow of water, slippery thing –
    trout, salmon
    otter, eel.
I am the sky, the air, the spring
I am the fish and the water
I am the soil under my feet, I am
    God and Man
Star in the midst of the highest stars,
    of that perfected brightness
I am the bird, I am the beast
    of fur and feather
birdlike beast, original
conceptions swelling in my skull
    as life in shell of egg
Soul, will, intellect of trout
Soul, will, intellect of shrub
Soul, will, intellect of man
    man and universe.

Translated from the Irish by Todd Hearon

Adam White   *Time-lapse Photographer*

I photograph ice – or the death of it.
I have cameras aimed at Alaska,
Montana, Greenland, Tibet, etcetera,

wherever thick floes are softening
at full tilt. I have no choice but to work
through the heart-searching dirt of it.

As a child, drawing houses with cars parked
outside and the factory where my father was,
I cried because I hadn't

one crayon the true colour of ice,
until my mother consoled me:
'Look, it's already there. Just draw around it.'

And what would you say to console me now?
when coal-fired holes etch the crest of the world,
and soot slicks into crevasse and melt-lake,

drawing a black shroud over the ice?

Derek Mahon   *World Trade Talks*

'Think globally, act locally.'

A 'Hindu growth rate',
hedges against the winds
of corporate finance; organic crops
and comely maidens, is it too late
to push for these demands
and pious hopes?

The great Naomi Klein
condemns, in *The Shock Doctrine*,
the Chicago boys, the World Bank and the IMF,
the dirty tricks and genocidal mischief
inflicted upon the weak
who now fight back.

A hare in the corn
scared by the war machine
and cornered trembling in its exposed acre,
a sacred thing projected on the moon
when the full moon is clear,
survives the roar

by lying low
in the heart-winnowing breeze.
Next spring, when a new crop begins to grow,
let it not be genetically modified
but such as the ancients sowed
in the old days.

Peter Gill   *Late Romantic*

The blue smoke rises above the plum trees
Beyond the garden into the autumn air.
There is no weather there without a season in it.
There are no rainy Saturdays just as
There are no railway sidings and no trains.
There is sobbing in the dark and the agony of young men
But always in the context of an appropriate time.

Inside there is everywhere the breath of comfort
Women's voices with a gloss on them like silver
Dispel the melancholy riding on the light.
Men provide enough anxiety to suit the purpose
Clever sisters sit at their work.
My heart is full, my heart is full of you.
This to the young girls.

The spirit that they find then living in the forests
The spirit that they find, walking, in the mountains
Fills the young men with abstractions of such beauty
That offers reparation to their kind.
Would take the world's pain as their own
But find safety in the house under the shabby limes,
Shun the white salons and the woodman's hut to go
Where there is forgiveness for sneering and young style.

And when the new time comes that they felt for
Find in the garden still the old world defined.
The smoke rising from the burning leaves
The smoke rising above the plums lying on the ground
is a sign of all that has been done.

Macdara Woods   *Lobelias: Achill Island*

for Donald Sur

A thousand flowers
lit up
the accidental roads

And dancing blue lobelias
just now
upon the window-sill

That brought us here
wherever
here is now –

Tip-step me into suddenness
my copper
nerves stripped bare

Cool blue plaster
clusters
round the feet of saints

At sight of sea and land
beyond
the sea and further tumbling sky

In empty childhood
country
churches long ago

Repeated land and sky
and layers
of sea and land and sky again

Or green hydrangeas
in country gardens –
blue copper verdigris:

Unending green all blue
all colours
breath – all movement all

Korean blue and green
make up
one colour kept for nature

All colours
flow
all colours – all

Blue and green
together –
Chung Sun told me this:

all movement air
until

all colour
green and blue

Denise McSheehy   *The Opening of the Veranda was*
                      the Beginning of Summer

All winter it lay dormant
a dump for mud-caked boots and bikes

the summer things, garden forks, deckchairs
buckets and spades inert and clammy

the rest of the house withdrawn
into the sealed red dark of the back room.

What was it I liked so much –
the glass roof a trap for sky and insects

how the glass could make days longer
signal change

the weathered garden door leaking raw
spring air, the holiday feel

of doors being open, morning coming in
yellow and buzzing.

When it stifled
a place to escape through – best

in the halfway season
watching the rain fall

in big splashes, the smell
of wet mud from the balding lawn –

pausing
before entering the house again.

Miriam Darlington   *Flora (a minor deity)*

On the first day she drew the anatomy of her heart
and superimposed it upon a piece of overgrown wilderness;

on the second day she wound the weeds round and round
herself so that the earth was bare and she was green;

on the third day she walked over the naked soil
sewing a careful tapestry of seeds;

on the fourth day she doused for springs, exposed them
and strengthened their outpouring with granite and rocks;

on the fifth day she brought in children to plant soft fruits of their choice
and advise about lawns and hiding places;

on the sixth day she did not rest because every woman knows
if you take your eyes off a garden for a minute it can go out of control –

on the seventh day earthworms, snails, insects, lizards and weasels came,
followed by many birds; on that day God made a surprise visit,

and on his way out he left the gate open, and afterwards they found
he had left his shoes.

Alison Brackenbury *Poppy Seeds*

Yes, they go everywhere, like breath.
They lodge in nails. They sweeten teeth

strange food to me. Are they that haze,
red banks, once corn's, now motorways

or from some special flowers? I read
our newborn brain knows what we see

but not the words. So that is learnt
as these seeds, skilfully, were burnt.

Oh, but I knew this. Before school
I spoke birds' nests, the blackbird's cool

mud, spoke eggs, the robin's scrawl.
1 robbed no nest. The words took all.

Black seeds, the sweet sleep under grief,
give me the language of the leaf.

Jeanette McCullough

Alice Oswald　　*Birdsong for Two Voices*

A spiral ascending the morning,
climbing by means of a song into the sun,
to be sung reciprocally by two birds at intervals
in the same tree but not quite in time.

A song that assembles the earth
out of nine notes, and silence.
Out of the unformed gloom before dawn
where every tree is a problem to be solved by birdsong.

Crex crex corcorvado,
letting the pieces fall where they may,
every dawn divides into the distinct
misgiving between alternate voices

sung repeatedly by two birds at intervals
out of nine notes, and silence.
While the sun, with its fingers to the earth,
as the sun proceeds so it gathers instruments:

it gathers the yard with its echoes and scaffolding sounds,
it gathers the swerving away sound of the road
it gathers the river shivering in a wet field,
it gathers the three small bones in the dark of the eardrum;

it gathers the big bass silence of clouds, as if your eyes had ears
it gathers the mind whispering in its shell
and all trees, with their ears to the air,
seeking a steady state and singing it over till it settles.

Gerard Smyth   *The Blackbirds of Wilkinstown*

It is spring now and it must be lovely down in
Wilkinstown. Are the birds singing yet? When you
hear a blackbird think of me.
– Francis Ledwidge

There's a village where nothing has changed for years,
sweet pastures through which the railway track
is a memento kept as part of the scenery;
the bog where bog work was a tug-of-war,
and Ledwidge's blackbird flaunted her song.
The gatekeeper's cottage is gone, no need now
for the gatekeeper's morning and evening vigil.
The trees are like trees in a Russian novel –
tall and gaunt, some ready to fall
in the next winter storm. The righteous
have their inner sanctum: the country chapel
where they pray for the bride at the altar,
the soul in the box. No spectacle ever intrudes
except when the blackbirds arrive.
Through the sweet pastures, meeting ground
of the harriers, it's a short walk
from schoolhouse to cemetery where husbands
and wives are resting in peace
and stone walls keep a little of the sun's day-warmth
for night that comes darkening the harvested fields.

Peter Branson   *Angels*

The Swallow (*Hirundo rustica*)

They move with speed and grace, charm insects on
the wing, style acrobats, the consummate
design. As ribbons dance in zephyr hair,
tails streamers draw the eye, to slip the leash
of everyday, weave four dimensions out
of three, re-jigging tousled sky. Nests dry
stone wall, last winter's ravage easy fixed,
these will o'wisp, zigs-zags of doppel shade
and light, like careless skaters on thin ice,
kiss mirror images in shallow stills.
The throat an open wound young suckle on,
they're gone before you know, these semi tones,
grace notes on telephone staves, to hibernate,
the story goes, like bats, in hollow boles.

Donald Sheehy   *At the Cliffs of Moher*

From 'Four Auguries'

Among sightseers peering down
the sheer steep wall of Thomond,
I overheard an Irishman whisper
of seabirds in their skeins below:

'Ah, will you look at them?' sighed he,
'Flyin' just for the love of it!'
—And kept aloft, I silently mocked,
on draughts of Irish rhetoric.

But his sooth said circles me yet.
And now in the mind's middle-distance,
at the brink between fall and asleep,
I hear the wind and the waves resound:

'Ah, just for the love of it,' he cries,
'Will you look at them flyin'!' And then
kittiwakes, petrels, and puffins ascend,
and scatters of stonechats chatter of home.

Seamus Hogan   *Heron, West Cork*

Among reeds
Surrounded by waves of rock,
Stands a Heron.
In its beak
The X of a frog
About to make his final 'plop!'

The Heron collects,
Beak first, then out around the wings,
Slowly, slowly all the way down, down
To its claw tips.
Slowly. Slowly drawing the cloak that is Heron
Up, up into air.

Seamus Hogan   *Territory*

Before settling for the evening
A cock pheasant
Hammers in staves of sound.

Then applauds himself.

After a pause
Smaller birds
Trellis the in-between spaces.

Peter Van Belle   *The Invention of God*

We know beyond our eyes
The raven folds its wings in flight,
Hurtles down like a dark star
Then soars towards the sun.

We know beyond our eyes
Fish backs give off haloes
Swimming down a sun's cathedral
Beneath the water's shimmer.

We knew, beyond our eyes,
So sought one that would see all,
For we thought these wonders
Wasted on mere beasts.

Hammond Journeaux

155

Abigail A. Zammit   *Cuyabeno in Four Movements*

The jungle hoists its music into a sky
whose light is a billion stars. Owl is perched
above the river, weighing its silence against
the flame of life beneath the undergrowth
where water tinkers, teases, pretending to sleep.
A watchful caiman pops its eyes above the surface.

Somewhere, between tree and water, the answer
spreads like a ripple. Instantly, the split
of cartilage and the caiman is jaws and teeth.
Tarantula dances madly to the rush,
the splurge of blood. Hurry whilst the killing
is pure! Tu-who! Tu-whit! Tu-who! This rhythm
is fur and claws. Cobweb tight as a trill.
Jungle dark is a screech, is a snap.

One by one, anacondas slipping from branches,
splashed music and blur. Piranhas a frenzy
of feed and song, frogs wail across twigs,
phosphorescence. Rhythm is root and pulse.
Pink dolpin rises to breathe. One eye, open.
Open, one eye, and the answer is milliseconds.
Shaman screams inside his speckled dream.

A millisecond owl's blink. And now
the shriek of the last cricket that will not rest.
Air heavy with rain and droplets where night
hides its feathery secrets. Squirrel monkeys
have fought themselves to sleep. Anacondas return
to their branches, hushed music and blur.
River is echo, is drip and ripple, twigs
tickle the surface. Sky blushes, coughs its last stars.

Cuyabeno is a nature reserve in Ecuador and part of the Amazon

156

Mary Turley-McGrath   *Shiftings*

The sky is a concave blue canvas
where the painter has dabbed
a twist of white in the cool air.

By the river bank, the salley bends,
broken, black and desultory.
A water-hen flicks from the sedge
and darts further up the river.

Rows of dead reeds line the grass
as far up as the hawthorn ditch.
In one pile, a black plastic oar
lies hidden. Half the blade is gone.

I carry it with me; it will stop
a gap in a hedge or prop open
a shed door. It will never feel the rush
of river but succumb

to a new element, like the carcass
of the dead newborn lamb, hidden
near furze in the Slough Field;
its wool and outer body perfect,

but eyes and ribcage empty,
picked clean by fox and crow;
hooves smooth, legs splayed
as if resting from a frolic.

WEATHER

Tony Weston   *No Fault of Mine*

Winter is no fault of mine, Lady –
Winter walks his own boots through the house.

No, I prefer, by far, the moment apple blossom
flirts its lifted skirts at every bee,

or when the sun pours molten metal
on every living corpse stretched on the beach

and Autumn's not so bad, if one likes apples
and fingers black and blue with hedgerow fruit –

but Winter, no, with dark and ice and snow
and stamping in as if he owned the place.

Seth Crook   *January Gales of Mull*

High winds tilt the tree tops now.
What is loose will tumble.
Low moods lean to feel the fire's glow,

and grumble. Slates may slip,
as minds unhinge like rotted gates.
What's not flown far will rattle.

Lips numb. Salt rips.
We'll stare until the last wood burns,
blink, blank-eyed like cattle.

Gerard Lee   *Snow*

Talk of snow thickened
in the children's dreams.

* * *

With the suddenness of an apparition
it was there, ghost-calling as it fell
to come out
come out if you dare.
But like the little porridge pot
it forgot to stop
and time skidded slowly to a halt.

* * *

Tramped ice compacted to a compound fracture finish,
while the plaster of Paris encasing the broken city
suffered a smudge of signatures;
vanilla speckle of dog's jet,
bird shits' corroding rust,
batik trails of blood.
Print of paw, claw, and cautious sole
of every starving thing that ventured out
during that week of going nowhere.
(And on the canal the swan mutely implored her etheric double
to set her free).

* * *

Seven days and seven nights held
the city's filth, till thaw's first sludge
(for here is my glove that was lost but is found)
unlocked the grime of snow's aftermath.

Clocks back in business then
the children went to bed to dream of more.

Stephanie Conybeare   *Undertow*

Something pulls.
It lies beneath.
The evidence is slight at first.

There's seepage.
Carpets spring damp patches.
Water gathers in dark corners
of disused rooms, and high-tide marks
appear on freshly painted walls.
It's when fishes are heard
in the eaves

dreams begin.
The mind at night is awash
with tidal waves bearing inland
mermaids, molluscs, sperm whales, sting rays,
selkies, octopodes and starfish
in a universal flood
of companionable sea life.

One morning, on awakening,
there's a gentle rocking motion,
a sweet sense of drift   .
before the strange discovery
that the house is on the move,
singing in its timbers,
following the course

of its river, deep below ground,
ocean bound.

Noel King   *Fisherman*

He had left her at home
waiting to cook a salmon supper
                              or a trout.
Since his stroke
he couldn't steady the hooks,
often sliced finger skin.
Another fisherman found him
slumped at the footbridge;
                              alerted the wife.
Her hands went straight
for an antiseptic to soothe his cuts,
scales of fish clinging,
and the smell of the river
                              lingering

Noel King   *The Fisherman's House*

His cap became a kneeler
when he blew-started the fire
at darkness. On June nights
when he didn't return until late
he still lit it, warming the walls for the night;
lit it from instinct; comfort from and for
his ancestors, knowing they needed it;
that it kept evils away.
Some nights he cooked at the fire,
toasting bread on a long fork,
boiling an egg in a bean can.
Then he would read a while;
May to October – light fiction,
deeper literature in winter.
By two in the morning he was sleeping.

Janis Mackay   *Faith*

Here they come, the ancient wives of the drowned departed,
Married now to salt wind, memory, the great rhythm of season
And incoming tide.

They throw their scraps to their drowned fishermen, their kin
Winged now after the northern sea change.

The gull frantic sea air over the pier cries at their croonings;
'we've hud wir denner, it's your turn love,
take that Jackie, you always liked chicken wings
when you came home frae the sea,'

to their drowned translated
feathered men.

Luis Fanti

Alana Farrell   *Sandown Beach*

The sea between the sand and sky's
the milky blue of a blind eye. As if
the water, lacking sight, has to feel

its way up the land's body
with its hands; stealing the strength of the moon
to slide its white fingertips up sands

that deepen to ochre on touch. It lies
like a lover, beached, skin to skin – high
tide, gasps – lets go the grains of the land.

In that long, slow and lovely turning
of the light to indigo, there she goes,
the sea, glows, flushing like a girl.

Peadar O'Donoghue

164

Kevin Kiely *On the Edge of the Ocean*

sky-
airbrushed white
by the fuel stream of two jets
this cold sunny day

who wants the land
the woods and weekend traffic
all is being told
on the edge of the ocean

the antique heron
wings full stretched
on a plinth of water-glazed rock
in a swell beyond the drilling waves
their near and far off thunder-

detonations of war

the watery nerves of the tide
stretch, strain and break
in hoops of surging foam
folding and unfolding
shorewards and seawards

each sun glistening pebble
drowned and saved
under the veil of lace
across the shingle

all is washed
to the whitest pebble
sucked sweetly
among the playful dogs
who lick and drink salt water

Atar Hadari   *Rowers in the Dusk*

A yellow light and then a golden
falls on the water and then a red
at that hour, carrying boat stools
and paddles the rowers go in to wade
carrying sculls with them and sometimes
entire crews carry one hull
and they take boots off once they are inside her,
they settle their feet on the trestle and put on shoes;
settle to row before last light
turns all their bodies to blue and the water cold;
finally somebody says 'Let's,'
'We're wasting light,' somebody calls and they leave the dock
half a score arms pulling one way
against the river, sometimes as they return they have the tide;
and golden they coast the water with light,
they turn to a body of ochre between the tide and sky,
turn to a torrent of shade over the water
part blood, part boat metal, part pure gold
and pulling they come back as night falls all purple
all black as the moon comes out,
sometimes stars twinkle in their water like dropped cigarette ash
but some moments just before dark they were pure light and sweat
and pulling the boat into harbour
they shake off the last heat of gold
and walk onto night's earth
for all that false light can give
and hands can steal from death.

Gerald Dawe   *Solo*

On days like these I often think
of Patrick Smyth on his boat,
cuffing through the waves
between Rathlin and Portrush,
lord of all he sees –
                 the coast of Ireland,
jagged and proud, shuns the north sea,
the seals and porpoises follow him
as he veers west to Malin Head,
a luxury liner rolls on the distant tide
and Patrick Smyth, alone on his boat,
with tables and maps, adjusts the sail
like a paper boat, a solo man
in all the wide wide sea.

Hammond Journeaux

John Wedgwood Clarke   *Lightships*

The trawler crawls in
with night on its shoulders,
wings folded
in glittering holds.

Around the harbour
we talk our way
into the dark hatchings
of lobster pots.

We have reached one of many
points. The boat slides
between stone.
The lightships scatter and let go.

LAND

Seamus Heaney *The Boiling House*

Four doors: calves' house, the middle house, the boiling house, the
home house. In census terms, three outbuildings, one dwelling.
All under the one run of thatched roof, behind one whitewashed,
single-storeyed wall.

The boiling house was dug-out dark, peat-dry and oddly sound-
proofed, a storage place for bags of meal and grain. Once upon a
time it too had been dwelt in, before it knew the scullion life that
still seethed in its name.

Heating of gruel, boiling of brock, slop-renderings, washes, fowl-
feeds, pig swill, hot water for pig-killings, for scouring of churns
and pails, for extra pots on the crane on threshing days.

At the moment of a death (Romans believed) the soul resolved
into three. The *manes* went to Elysian Fields or deeper, to
Tartarus. The *anima* returned itself to the gods; and the *umbra*
hovered, unwilling to quit the body.

I am content with that. Now I know what haunted and hovered
there. In an old reluctant breath from behind the bags. In a pelt
of soot that trembled in the chimney. In the clay floor that stayed
obstinate and simple.

Gabriel Fitzmaurice   *Cutting Grass in Glenalappa*

In the name of all who went before us we cut this grass:

The ones who farmed the homestead,
The rest who emigrated
To become firemen, policemen and domestics in New York,

Factory workers and navvies in London, Leicester, Sheffield, Saint Helen's,
Thelwall, Dagenham, Walford.
In your name we cut this grass.

Know today, you're not forgotten
As my son and I cut the grass you cut before us
At home in Glenalappa.

In the name of your sons and daughters we cut this grass,
And their children
And their children's children;

And for the time when there's no Fitzmaurice left in Glenalappa,
When the family have scattered like seeds on the wind,
When all that's left here of the Fitzmaurice is green grass,

in the name of all those generations, today we cut this grass.

Dermot J. Archer   *Building Wall*

Something there is that does love a wall.

At Inishmore we archive this in his dry-stone walling.
He balances each burren boulder
As deftly as he would the *sliothar*.
But this is no game
Even if he has a contestant in the weather.

His ancestors knew why they built up stones.
The island's Dun Aengus fort
With its stepped wall, its *chevaux-de-frise*
Armoured in, butted out.

Here is no enemy.

It isn't as if he would make a field hospital
Isolating self-heal, herb robert, chamomile, field scabious
Or spell friend or foe
In a harebell domed concert hall
Featuring oystercatcher, ringed plover
The sedge warbler's cover version.

I ask him why he walls.
'To clear the land' he says.
Here there's no pasture, no cultivation.

It's stone he walls in.

The sliothar is the hard ball used in the game of hurling

171

Kate Miller   *In the Gaeltacht*

So, there are thirteen words for rain
in your tongue, tell me one to fit
the clumsy rush of wet
that whooshes up the lane
inflating and detaching

hedges' awnings, upsets
fuchsia's every red umbrella,
hurls slip-slop scoops of honeysuckle
and crams the mouths of field drains
with meadowsweet.

Will it do for up-flung
salted spray which whitens shoes,
rusts bikes, burnishes and buffs
tarmac to mirrors? Is it the same
for rain that sweeps the bay

to round up sea-mist
early on a summer morning,
and in the saddle of Mount Brandon
herds its water into corries,
out of sight? Have you the name

for one which whistles,
reedy, low, a tune that wakes us to no
field, no tideline, roof or peak
as while we slept it rained away
the world that called us to the window?

N. Daly   *The Old Hands*

The old hands laugh
at the new hands sat up
at the bar in knitted sweaters.

Men who don't understand
livestock or how to manage without clocks.

To them the new hands are useless
unable to hold a ram, keep a bee,
ring a bell or deliver a lamb.

The new hands laugh
at the old with their advice
about how to keep sane in a
close knit community with more sheep than people.

John Greening   *Glendalough*

Reflections we like: of trees
but not of ourselves skimming
flat words across the surface
of a Sunday. A hanging

valley we like, where water-
fall and the furred arteries
of the valley pump accompaniment
to a lost, unlikely psalming.

Ruins we like, and inaccessible
doors into a tower that points
towards the storm that never came,
then turns to a sun-dial. We like

the impossible height of its mica,
slate and granite jenga game,
the missing ladders and the silent
peal in its throat; and we like

the shadow sewn through our light
by the eye at the tip of the needle
that makes us think we like
to think of Heaven, though we

prefer what's on our mobiles.
Age we like: and old grey oaks
that won't act their age
but quell the acid fallacy

with lichen. And we like girls
striding remains of a monastic
city who last night were pretty
on bar-stools, with bare legs,

and the one observing Ramadan
who walks ahead in a veil
of hunger and takes the round
tower's bearing towards sunset.

Stephen Shields   *Salthill Evening, November*

Outside the café, rain
washes the promenade.
Next-door's broken chute heaves
a stream across the window.

That single ship
struggles to move along
the bay.

A mist,
dense as chain mail,
follows from the harbour,
grips the stern:

A touch of invisibility,
sure as that on forgotten
ferries to the islands,
black cows bawling in the hold,

or old cargoes
of outbound ore,
with a gloss on a grey flint
like the eye of a whale
before it sounds.

Paul O'Prey   *A Way Back In*

The pitted shore lost long ago
to the bungalow
the out of town store

but up here on a high wind
heavy with sea
the old deep chalk track sunk
across the long green curve rising
into the sky
into my own clear blue

still the place to come
when on the run

to stand like Adam at the gate of Eden
knowing what is lost
looking for a way back in

Susan O'Toole   *Homebound*

The Aum, diddle die story
Of the Westerland, Midland and Eastland,
Long Island, of it all.
The Nellie,
Lame leg and all of it
Walking with the Cows, to the deep drone of the Bull,
Along Westerland strand to eat grass
Sweetened by the salt spray of the Sea.
'Everything's in it, it's all they could ever want,' She chants,
Kneeling down to rest on the rocks in the moon-dusk.

Overhead, Island birds pilot the stars,
Above the Sea, soused in blue gull foam,
Drooling their wings homebound.
Below a sky studded with crystal stars,
Each one a light, mirrored in the Sea,
Becomes a rush of presence, where the moment is exiled
From the complementarity of opposites.
A hush flows from her breath, while a prayer quietly comes in
Washed-up from the heart, with the spray, and everything in it,
Weaving all together in one drop.
Its taste has all the freshness of the moment, in that spray,
is the Island,
A drop,
a light returning home,
a rhythm,
a ring of Aum,
Aum diddle,
Die story
of it all.

Peter Mabey   *The Holy Mountain*

They say you can't move mountains, but indeed they can move you

From Ahakista to Toormore, Durrus to Ballydehob
your black carapace hulks at night, making appear to float
above it your orange antenna which stalk
distant aircraft flying in from Boston and New York.

Like your Antipodean brother Fujiyama,
you are borrowed landscape, 'sensei'
for the yellow, pink and white homes who chose
to nestle between your copper-veined toes.

Many a conquering hero
has had his heart lifted
from the turn of the road at Ardurabeg
with a welcoming glimpse of your Olympian head.

Twin-eyed sentinel of the Mizen
impassively you've stood
surveying marauding pirates and Norsemen,
fisherman, ploughman, hurler and oarsman.

The wagon train of pink clouds
comes chugging in off the Atlantic
their soft underlimbs parted by your blunt nose
leaving you Bill Haley bangs of faintest rose.

Even as your namesake Gabriel
blew the water of life into the Mother Mary,
so you too feed the mountain streams
that give birth to a thousand hopes and dreams.

THE SHOp was published from a
cottage on the Holy Mountain
– Mount Gabriel, near Schull, County Cork.

Peter Mabey

Padraic MacCana   *Bird and Horse and Him and a Dark Road*

After walking a horse from God knows where
In he came and brought the night in with him,
Him so full of it he touched an ear
That loved the road, the horse, the lonely walker.

Above his head a bird had bleated, bleated;
Wing and hoof inspired awe and fear;
Bird and horse and him on a dark road;
He might have walked from a fair across the Border.

No light to break the dark road or a face,
Hoof-beats did it and the listening dark
And bleating, bleating over him that wing;
Hoof and wing and him on a lonely road.

Recalled long after by the listening ear
Who knew it wanted telling, wing and road,
The hoof, the wing, the walker and his awe
When horse and walker were below the sod.

And why did wing bleat, bleat, bleat over him
And made him tell it to a loving ear,
The lonely walker, hoof and road and awe
And the dark that clung to his lonely face and fear?

John McAuliffe   *The Street*

for John B. Keane

On the street, you wouldn't know what was just finishing,
Swept clean already of dockets and tickets, the mingled smell gone
Of cigars, straw, horses. Byrds lorries rumble out of town
Past late mass traffic, the odd mitching teenager and us, shopping
For the papers before we drive away home to Dublin. 12:15
And the whole clean town like a set that's been deserted,
The loudspeakers broadcast Radio Kerry to no-one.
A boy drizzles water into window boxes above the Archway,
A man puts a box accordion into the boot of his Datsun.

In Jet's the news is a man's stepped in front of the Cork train,
Might the match be delayed? Nobody can say.
The L&N's shop assistant is glad the week is gone:
'Now, at last, things'll quieten down. But ye're off anyway' –
She measures our life like a basket of shopping.
And we make out the days ahead: school traffic, the rustle of shops,
The street's habitual walkers, the wash of rumour, the drift
Of late-night talk of money made and lost, winter settling
In the street till it's black and white with rain and frost.

Denise Ryan   *Liberties Moon*

Forever eternal, the fireflies dash around my head:
rearranging my hair ornament, fluttering down my slide,
clasping a paper cone of happiness, pear drops and bullseyes.
The yawning sun stretches its lengthy rays
permitting me to lean on its tips.
Draped on a bollard of yellow butter,
the milkmaids throne among the council dwellings –
no daylight shines on the balcony's face
forever cold and dark wearing doors of different colours
like painted toenails on a black foot.
Behind the gate lies the metal wreck
that once took me to the moon and back
I discarded its wheels behind the pram shed
with the rest of the most wanted junk.
Awhile the daytime ghost drifts in the breeze,
displaying their smalls with such vitality;
soon the chimneys will cough up dust
and the sun will rest behind the back of the pipes,
falling into a sombre sleep from inhaling the Guinness fumes.
A drunken sun in a sober sky:
an image of the past forever present,
a commercial for innocence that sells every time.

Peter Redgrove   *Gentlemen*

The town Gents
                    flooded as usual
                                        by the chalice-fountain
Stained with birds;
                    I went down into this pit
                                        it was awash with libations,
Half-lit through knotted glass
                    set in the pavement overhead
                                        like a leaky battery
With stained plates and pungent packing
                    just large enough for a dozen pissers
                                        to piss nether electricity together;
Piss powerhouse
                    water playing over stone;
                                        so I climbed the stairs
From the one electricity to the other,
                    sunlight winged with doves, wings,
                                        and all the hearts beating together
In the keels of their breastbones
                    like winged ships,
                                        rainwater off wings
And wings astonished at Gents
                    rising out of the ground;
                                        I climbed from one fragrance
Into another,
                    the hiss of the feathers,
                                        the piss of the men
Men ascending and praising the sunlight,
                    the water-carriers, the men descending
                                        into the charged twilight, then up
To fill their eyes with water off stone,
                    water sunlit with dove-wings,
                                        visible electricity,
Water that gives us sight,
                    passes through, hisses,
                                        rests in the head-bone fountain
where the whole scene swims.

Siobhán Duffy   *Piss*

For fuck's sake I muttered
Under my breath
While steering the buggy
And my good boots out
Of the path of the stream of his warm piss
Making a river on the pavement
Which all the shoppers from Penneys
Had to ford in his wake.

His jeans still unbuckled and
Loose, still tucking in his shorts
Against the wall,
Where all the mothers and children and fathers
Could see him stumble
And zip himself up.

Disgust, was what I felt.
Not a thought gave I to
What might have brought
Him to this moment,
What road he might have taken to
Arrive at this one
Overwhelming urge
That shut out
The rest of the world.

Mary Durkin   *Wolves*

Look, among grey Peabody housing, cradled
low between two main-line stations, the streets are
gently lit. Here, safe behind stained metal bars,
sheltered by shutters,

corner shops sell newspapers, milk and alcohol
sweetened for children. Here in these streets, banked by
embankments, I watched as three wolves prowled, softly,
prowled round the street lights.

All the other noises were far off (there was
glass breaking somewhere, a siren). I could
hear the warm mouths nuzzling piles of black bags
heaped in the gutters,

feel the smooth paws, silk on the flagstones. Three wolves
moved by, fanned out, one to bite into street rags,
one to piss, and one to watch. These are not my
wolves. Whose wolves are these?

These streets are ruled by hooded boys with shiny
eyes and polished breath who will sleep by day and
carry knives to fight through the night. I know the
hooded boys all right.

Three wolves remain. Their coats are coarse and warm, their
breath is rich and damp, their eyes dull yellow, slight, like
winter flowers, like aconite, monkshood, that
grows in mountain regions.

Peter Salisbury   *Three Frames*

i. Aston Quay

Suits stand at an open window
relaxed in formal wear,
headless cravats, legless tails,
in idle conversation with the waves
blown upriver.

An oak leaf falls
on the page.

ii. Ormond Quay

I count
a full round
of the Angelus,

as the cormorant dives
long enough for ripples to form
circles and fade
into leaves and fag butts
floating downriver.

iii. Inns Quay

The day is an empty bedroom, windows open,
linen drawn back and aired.

On the boardwalk, where the homeless meet,
tourists sit with coffee

folding their maps. Two swans cross the Liffey
focused on a Spanish girl's camera.

C.M. Millen   *Red Letter Day*

Christ they had to be carried out of Gallagher's
after having God knows how many
after they'd been up to the doctor in Swinford
and celebrating, ninety-two years on.
Jesus, they were mad with the drink
and smokin' the odd fag,
though they were not, as a habit,
smokers,
but all the same
chimneys they were that night
and the stories came out of them, one after the other,
like the ram with ewes in heat,
the stories came, from both Bridie and May, twins you know,
and toasts, Jesus, toasts go leor.
To May's son, the priest, in Baltimore,
and their father, God bless him, fifty years now dead
and to the photo of the Sacred Heart
over the back of the bar, illuminated,
and, Jesus, best of all, to the *Catholic Messenger*
which came every month, with the Lord's words
printed in red.

For that red ink,
that they would wet with their spittle
and smear on their cheeks
to use as the rouge
their father never
let them wear.
Oh, Jesus, even well after they were carried out
ninety-two years and twins,
it was falling over laughing,
doubling over laughing,
we were still.

Patrick Cotter   *Stolen*

What has happened to the two-headed holy water font
carved over twelve hundred years ago from local limestone,
embedded in a graveyard wall for mere decoration
after the Reformation? Those monkish heads saw William's
army besiege Elizabeth Fort. Musket balls whined past
their faces then. The Croesus-rich Chattertons paraded
their coffins past on the way to their mausoleum two
centuries ago. Philandering couples canoodled
beneath the font's four nostrils obscured by wild clematis.
How did they judge the smell of pert youth?

Last century I tore back the undergrowth so the heads
could view again the cloudy/blue skies over St Maries
of the Isle, how the Ideal Menswear factory bustled
with industry. Now they've gone and no one knows where,
now when the factory is silent, the girls are thinning
in numbers while widening in girth, and the old nuns no
longer cover up their chaste greying locks with black wimples.

Last century on summer nights with star-riddled skies I
slept in a fluorescence of untrimmed shoots sprouting four feet
tall 'round the base of the great elm's bole. The heads adjacent
kept the demons of the surrounding graves at bay; the souls
of the never-satisfied who died well before ready,
their names obscured by weathering on headstones halfsunk
from the subsidence of centuries. The blackbirds trilled their
shrill alarm as I awoke and strode through the stalks of wild
raspberries. But what alarm sounded when some bastard stole
the holy water font with two heads, like some underloved
double-headed foetus sharing one heart? Two heads – my friends.

Patrick Cotter and the Two-Headed Holy Water Font, 1987

Rebecca Gethin   *No Pretence – 1746*

Our paying guest slept with a loaded pistol
beside his pillow – seldom spoke
but understood our Gaelic.

He wore a Highlander's kilt: odd, those bare knees.
All day he watched from a headland,
wrapped in a plaid, gusts whipping his eyes.

We shared the little we had,
warmth of peat, dish of mackerel,
gulls' eggs, but he shook his head at poteen.

Hands white as a dairymaid's skin –
wore rings on his drawing room fingers
unroughened by farm work or hauling nets.

When a ketch took shelter
he was heard speaking some language
to crewmen who rowed ashore, fetching water.

When wind veered the ship sailed south
and, without a word, he was gone.
Soon after, Mother's scrofulous neck healed.

She remembered how three times
he'd stretched his hand to stroke her shoulder.
She always said she'd been touched by a king.

John McGrail   *1833: The Hedge-Schoolmaster's English*
Lesson for Emigrants

They are like unto children sitting in the marketplace,
and calling one to another and saying
We have piped unto you, and ye have not danced;
we have mourned for you, and ye have not wept.
(Luke 7:32)

We skirled the *uileann* for ye,

But divil a step of *damhsa*.

We tootled the *feadóg*

firninst your ears,

howled the *caointe*,

and what *gol* was there?

uileann – pipes
damhsa – dance
feadóg – flute
caointe – dirges (keening)
gol – weeping

Michael Casey   *Fever Sheds*

Having escaped the fever sheds,
She lies on the damp grass of Grosse Ile.
After months below deck, she wants to die
In open air, under familiar stars.
Memory burns: her youngest boy buried
at sea, the small weighted body sinking
slowly, waves closing over him.

On entering the St Lawrence, pilots
fixed a blue flag to the fore top-gallant
masthead to signal fever. Too late for her,
though, God willing, her husband
and daughters will be allowed
ashore at Quebec; she will never know.
What if no one survives the coffin ship?

The last gulls of evening slice sideways
through the dark sky, and cold prowls
the island like a hungry wolf. There are stars,
the scent of wild violets and an overhanging
maple tree. But a fallen star had poisoned
the world with the sweet smell of rot, and four
horsemen were let loose upon the land.

Michael McKimm   *The Land League*

The Geological Survey in Ireland

Hard to keep one history from another,
but he kept his head low, used simple tools:
notebook and pencil and a good pair of boots,
and a lunch prepared in the boarding house
if the landlady was willing, which they
usually were, this being official scientific business.

Today, day three at the Gweebarra Fault.
Moorlands; heather and moss; bold naked
granite bursting through. He took the path
along the widening lake to Glenbeagh,
learned from Mrs Adair about the last red
deer to leave Co. Donegal, not long back.

'Did you learn,' they'd ask him later in the pub,
'about Mr Adair, forcing out them families,
most now dead.' Hard to counter their talk
of agitation and freedom with limestone,
or to explain how a glacier rolled down
this valley, flexured and folded the land.

Margaret Holbrook   *Dinorwig, 1900. The Slate Miner*

He removed the hat, shook it.
It was winter wet with melted snow.
He thought of his father, how he'd worn this hat.

He took a cloth and wiped it damp dry.
His father's face there, clear in his mind.
He rolled up pieces of newspaper and
as he pushed them into the crown,
it was his father's hands he saw.

He placed the hat by the hearth to dry completely.
Tomorrow he would attend to the brass buckles
until they shone. And the leather once dry,
would be polished, buffed, weather proofed.

'You have to look after it, see,' his father
always said. He could hear the words plain as day.
He'd never really left him, had he?

And as he looked at the hat drying by the fire,
memories returned. He knew it was good
to be home and safe from the day.

Noel Conneely   *Liberty Hall*

Liberty Hall climbs in cloud and the fingerprints
of the age are all over Pearse and Connolly
as they stash their weapons in the basement.
They are waiting for a signal from Butt Bridge
but the signaller is up in the White Horse
hands cupped around a ball of malt by the fire.
Further up where the river tries to escape,
the Winding Stair that creaked so beautifully,
disappears as a window of opportunity opens
and the timber gives way to the culture.
A woman in a black coat takes the air on Eden Quay
and the inebriated evening hums a tune
she doesn't know the name of.
The sound of guns from the GPO and down in the FSC
workers search the web for holiday options.
The blood of martyrs reds their wellies.
Wagons emerge from the rubble and smoke in Sackville Place,
where a taximan takes another fare
and Volunteers who make it up Abbey Street
are shot at the abbey's door.

Deirdre Brennan   *The Rector's Daughters*

A grey nineteenth century day,
the sea-swell grey under somber cliffs;
two sisters in a row-boat, small stick figures,
beneath a swooping wreath of gulls
tow a trawl of seaweed, jelly fish, wafers of bone,
secrets of the empty carapace they will probe,
sit up late by lamplight, aching with the need
to name, label, paint in the most careful detail.

Sticking to the known to sift the unknown,
they never go missing like their brothers
in African jungles or Arctic ice; knowing,
as they do by heart, the salt marshes of home,
drainage creeks where coastal and inland
vegetation merge, wildfowl and rabbits graze;
where keen as oyster-catchers, in the shore-wash
they gather here a fish-fin, there a fanned shell.

On the headland, the local women spread
seaweed and sand on a lime-starved scatter
of potato fields, bleach their dull washing
on fuchsia hedges, sort slates in slate quarries,
suckle children, bury them, beget more,
watch the daft goings on of the Rector's daughters,
without as much as a husband or child between them,
breeding family after family of jellyfish in glass jars.

Julian Farmer   *Spenser's Optics*

Mr Spenser was a physicist.
Working in the mountains
on one invention or another,
he would drive down to teach his class.

Trolleys with tickertape,
cloud chambers, Leyden jars
and Vandergraph generators
buzzed with insight, glinted love.

A pin was set up
on a calibrated board,
lit, projected through the dark
and a well-ground lens.

A focal length of twelve
$1/v = 1/f - 1/u$
$m = v/u$ and the image was
ninety millimetres high.

So, there we were – at fifteen.
We had seen into the eye of life
and ridden on the astral motion
of science and philosophy.

The Almighty had waved at us –
light threading through transparencies
to deposit new ideas
with its even-handedness.

And that is the reason
(Papist though I am)
that I will always honour
the Enlightenment.

WAR

Brendan McMahon   *War*

Those who are deaf to tears must endure
the knife's voice, and the gun's shout at the window.
Real wars are fought for colours, the green
or cruel red, the black against the white.

Those who are blind to grief must look upon
its image, see the pale and broken face forever.
Real wars are fought for number, the Many
and the Three in One, the Even and the Odd.

Those who cannot touch the lost must face
eternities of ice and loneliness.
Real wars are fought for love, their battleground
the body, and the bleeding human heart.

Mark O'Flynn   *The Allotropes of Tin*

(for Roy Tasker)

Unbeknownst to him
it takes a chemistry lesson
to decipher the shreds of fabric left in snow.
Absent tin tells us more than tin;
cloth more than fossil
when the Spring thaw melts
to reveal history's diet of bones.
Certainly the neatest looking army in the field
Napoleon's men march towards the cold,
not knowing the compound elements
of French tin will crystallise at less than five degrees.
As coal to diamond, all those tin buttons
shining on the parade grounds of Paris,
who could imagine defeat
beneath the sun's benevolence?
By the time they reach the Russian Winter
the smart, tin buttons, yes, have crystallised,
corroded and crumbled from the uniforms
of Napoleon's sublime advance.
His men fight to hold their trowsers up,
clutch their uniforms together
let alone aim a shivering musket
at an enemy laughing in the distance.
Their defeat creeps upon them like a mould.
Coal to diamond; love to hate; loyalty to despair;
flesh and the rot within the flesh.
The allotropes of tin slowly vanquish
an emperor, leaving their clues,
stripped of all ambition now,
naked arses fleeing,
cooling quickly under the warm snow.

Dan McFadden   *The Memory of Snow*

There is only one step from the sublime to the ridiculous
— Bonaparte, 1812

He was unearthed by road workers digging out the roundabout for a new
   trunk road in Vilnius.
He leapt out in his rags of grand armée braid swearing in antique French
   they couldn't comprehend.
The Polish foreman took him gently aside, dosed him with coffee,
Discreetly phoned for the police, who at a loss, put him on a train to
      Paris.
Packed into a carriage with hopeful emigrants who shared their food and
   asked his name.
He stared back in silence all the way home.
Where he wandered up and down looking for his favourite café. It could
   not be found.
In the end he sat on the steps outside Notre Dame until darkness fell.
   It began to snow.
In the swirl of the flakes he saw again the scarecrow columns, the frost-
      bitten feet.
How victory had turned into defeat, that city, their refuge became their
   tomb.
He walked to the banks of the Seine, curled up on a bench,
Wrapped in his ragged greatcoat. Ice crystals formed on his face.
 A thaw at dawn left nothing. Wet city streets, the memory of snow.

Anne Haverty *Forgetting*

About a distant place, he said that
since the war they're all depressed
and with a grim philosophy – or flip –
I thought, well, whether you're guilty or
bereft, you can't bring back the dead,
what can they do but go on, forget?

But remembered the land around Ypres –
those old killing-fields of the killer years
smoothed over with pretty villas and roads,
kids yanked from a killing-game on screen
to be driven reluctantly to piano class
– the ghosts smothered under the grass.

Was it pointless too my horror then at
how easy it seems to go on, forget?

Mark Roper *John Condon*

Little statistic, lost in the ledger
of this century's slaughter, you fled
the stink and intimacy of Teapot Lane
to enlist at Clonmel. Wrangled your way
into a draft for France. Lasted one week.
It seems, at fourteen, you were the youngest
of the millions to die in that war.
Killed May 1915, Bellevarde Ridge.

How high it would rise above you, how
it hides you, ridge of that war's dead.
Number's all we can trick you out in:
1 week. 14 years. 1st World War. Millions.
One star burning in the dark of a well.
Fourteen white flowers on an apple branch.
The first swallow's skimming return.
In a poppy capsule, a million seeds.

Eamon Lynskey *Kristallnacht on the Late Night Bus*

When thugs fell out among themselves upstairs
on the late-night bus from town I knew then
why it was that everyone kept quiet
when the cattle trucks went rumbling past, full –
and quieter still when they came back later, empty

And when threats ran out and knives were drawn
and two drunks fought together in the aisle
I knew then how it was that people bought
the children's clothes, and shoes were put on sale
outside the camps; how uniformed gangsters

ruled the streets at will and forced old men
to scrub the kerbs before they smashed their heads.
When bottles smashed across the chromium bars
and showered their brittle specks of coloured glass
across the heaving floor the blood froze

in our faces and the only thing
that anyone could wish for at that moment
and above all else this world might offer
was just one clear run across the aisle
and down the swaying staircase. When the bus

lurched sideways to a halt and all the louts
gave up their enemies to fight against
whatever representative of law
had come to tackle them – what could match
our abject, coward relief? What kristallnacht

could match our terror on that late-night bus
from town when seats were ripped apart and who
dared look was spat on? Deep within we felt
the stir of something sharp and forked, a thing
to paralyse a thought, a thing to stop the heart.

Clare McCotter   *The Night Train*

after *Man's Search For Meaning, by* Viktor Frankl

At about midnight they passed
through a Viennese station
some standing some squatting in shifts
over scanty sodden straw.

From a crack in the dark side
of a cattle car he sees only night juddering
over the street where he lived
as a man and as a boy.

Onward toward the blue Danube
their breathless bones wait
for that first bridge crossing
straight to the heart Mauthausen.

Passing it by exhalations escape
out through a thin slatted hour
the relief an aria
in black Bavarian night.

Rousing angels from rapture
to watch words on wintered breath
Dachau only Dachau only Dachau
plough a furrow to the stars.

Daniel Daly   *Visit to Germany*

When Dresden was reduced to ruin
by firestorm worse than Hiroshima,
life seemed a place where hopelessness
began. Heil Hitler or Hail Mary
a milestone in the horror of our history.
Now in this harmony of restored monuments,
love may exist for us again, in metaphor at least.

The Alte Pinakothek in Munich:
concealed in a small glass cabinet
from colour-loss and fingernail
you may find in wonderment
Adam Elsheimer's Flight into Egypt.
Denial of freedom is another form of death.
Dachau, the camp from which no one returned,
seen in the city underground, a startling word
on a banal U-Bahn sign, a burning smell.

Ilya Kaminsky   *Fourteenth Week*

On the balconies, sunlight, on poplars, sunlight, on our lips.
Today no one was shooting, there is just sunlight and sunlight.
A girl cuts her hair with imaginary scissors –
A girl in sunlight, a school in sunlight, a horse in sunlight.
A boy steals a pair of shoes from an arrogant man in sunlight.
I speak and I say sunlight falling inside us, sunlight.
When they shot fifty women on Tedna St.,
I sat down to write and tell you what I know:
A child learns the world by putting it in his mouth,
A boy becomes a man and a man earth.
Body, they blame you for all things and they
Seek in the body what does not live in the body.

Sheila Hamilton   *Bread Oven in the Cantal*

Mouth-gape of stone in the garden.
A hot-spot, once.

I picture the makers of the bread:
women in this kitchen, kneading,
placing dough to rise
when Louis the Fourteenth is a young king,

with large paddle, lifting hot loaves
from the oven when rumour of a revolution comes.
They tap the bread to test its readiness.
Through wars: the energetic waving of flags,

the losses.
Also, quieter dramas:
slippery birth of a calf,
an apple-glut,
a visitor.

They agree
that the lynching of the German soldier
was not good.
They can understand it
but it was not good.

Mary Ellen Fean   *Basra, 2005*

The same sun we worship
Bakes the blackened streets
Burns the children's feet
(Small children, small feet)
Running from the guns –

Women searching
In bleeding fruit
And debris of what
Was the city market –

                    This is aftermath

Squad regroups, debrief,
High-five an absolution –
For dinner
Hamburgers
And American coffee,
In this land of coffee.

In desert night
They dream of home,
Mid-western towns,
In the ancient city.
The dead are counted,
(Women mostly)
And prepared for burial –

                    This is theatre

In the land
That gave us Superman
And Mickey Mouse
The commander fixes his tie,
Fixes his smile
For the evening news,
Begins, on cue
Good evening, my fellow countrymen

                    This is play

Ger Reidy *Between Wars*

From nowhere, a day without pain,
grateful, I kneel in the last pew,
beside a scattering of old women
the statues wait for the words we give them,
the angels want to drown us in peace.
This is how it must be after the armies retreat
and the dead are buried – the absence.

From the next street,
echoes of children left behind
who have made a football from a pig's bladder
before the common misery begins,
before we hear the roar of the engines,
before our boys accept shiny uniforms
and the churches fill again with mothers.

Michael Bartholomew-Biggs   *Cover-Up*

*A reproduction of Picasso's painting 'Guernica' at UN Headquarters
in New York was covered up during press briefings which
followed Security Council debates on Iraq in February 2003.*

Draw the curtains over Guernica.
On no account remember screaming horses,
let alone the howling mouths of children
and their mothers when the borrowed bombers
loomed and plunged. Too much illumination
here; the hand-clasped oil lamp; the flames;
a single filament still glowing as
the ceiling's falling. How can broken swordsmen
brandish pointed tongues at cameras
underneath that bloody naked bulb?

Deborah Tyler-Bennett   *Kumpania**

Move on, move on. *Roma* pass slabbed faces
as neighbours drive them on.
Band of ghosts, nothing to do
with this small town. Always someone watches
Roma as they're moved, moved on.
From any century, coats piled on carts with pots.
Years move on, these forced processions
aren't condemned. Winds blow
and on the footsteps go,
children swaddle plastic dolls,
mothers clutch embroidered shawls,
old men hobbling to their last small town.

Excuses surface, they must be moved on.
Superstition, hefty crow wheeling
above market places.
Blustering neighbours tell of curses,
soured milk ... illegal
parking.

Songs move on, this town's name listed
with unfriendly places. On and on,
songs from the *lungo drom*.
Civic hands reveal familiar cards:
resettlement and repatriation.
Small town Mayor shares plans
to house his Roma in a camp
some three miles out of town.
Always that refrain '*Move on, move on.*'
Behind his townsfolk, rows of ghostly guards,
cold hearts lamented by the *Roma* tongue,
another place name for *Papusza's* song.

* Kumpania: band of families; lungo drom: long road;
Papusza: gypsy poet/singer, 1940s

Joseph Horgan   *To Those Who Have Inherited Ireland*

If we'd known
We'd have stayed.
We could have lingered
Outside of your
Electronic gates,
Built your
Crowded motorways,
Instead of theirs.
You would have had no need
Of east European nannies
When there were so many
Slips of girls,
Slipping away.
Leaving home.
Ah, if only we'd known
We'd have stayed.

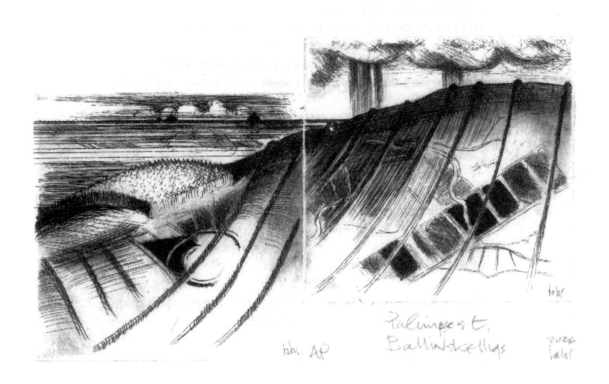

Palimpsest,
Ballinskelligs

AP

2026
lalor

Brian Lalor

Peter Wise   *A Man Speaks*

We turned to shore
with only sprats and bottom-feeders
to feed the village.
Even the herring had fled.
A boat came out of the grey light.
A warrior carrying a sword
called out:
Are you subjects of our lord the king?
Sir, I said:
we are fishermen.

I'd been walking for four days
when we came out of the wood.
The month was May.
I carried acorns in my pocket
to suck and chew.
Cars were stopped on the road.
A man asked:
Are your people Muslim or Croat?
Sir, I said:
we are musicians.

Harry Clifton   *A Flight Into Egypt*

Sixteen years we lived, among alien people,
Cities without bridges to be burned.
Uncertain roofs, protecting ourselves, a couple
Gone into hiding, who would one day return
When the balance of power changed, and the attitudes.
Meanwhile, strangers were kind. The terrible places,
Unexpectedly, were generous with food,
Indifferent for the most part, sometimes even gracious.
And to this day, our books on the shelf,
Our suitcases unpacked, I ask myself
If ever it might happen again –
Protection of innocence, Herod's dispensations,
Transit lounges, midnight railway stations –
No, not even whether, only when.

Michael Mackmin   *A Lean Year*

Snow on the sand, snow drifted against
grey waves, that mixture of pallors,
and the boat pulling towards the shore,
grounding and the boy out first running
with the rope to the waiting group,
the women, who haul the craft up the beach.
The weary rowers step out with their oars
and under the thwart a dark bundle.
The stillness as one carrying a lantern
steps forward. It is like some
etching of time past – darkening sky
lamplight on the faces making all there
suddenly young, eyes, mouths, hands,
the thick cloth wrapping against
the winds ice and disaster's dread.

Lastly the helmsman stepping ashore
lifting a child, a small babe, out of the boat
who wails at the storm, is alone
all that could be saved – the mother,
alive when found, gave up
as they hauled her into the boat.
No jubilation. Another mouth to feed
and this a hungry shore, a lean year.

But the boy now, his face turned windward,
begins suddenly, prompted by what strange
thought he never, years after, ever makes out,
begins to sing. Women step to hush him but
the one carrying the lantern says 'No, let him sing
let his song go up for all of us, let him sing'.

Thomas McCarthy   *Hiding Joseph in Ireland*

It is too complex now to be telling you the full story
And anyhow I know you and I know what you'll do:
You'll put Joseph in a poem just as we're all trying to
Help everyone to forget Joseph. He never lived here.
We don't know. We don't know. What does it matter
To you whether it was Rwanda or Burundi or Sudan,
Whether it was another small place in a pool of oil,
A place somewhere in Nigeria that caused Joseph
To flee. Does it really matter to you? I mean,
God forbid, you seem to understand only politics.
As for Joseph, let me tell you he can rhyme in his
Third language, better than you could ever do.
We loved the lecture you gave us on the Celtic poets,
How they spent seven years in apprenticeship. It
Was the same with Joseph. I don't wish to embarrass
You, but he spent seven years keeping a rhythm of exile,
And when he found his father, and two brothers,
Dismembered, covered in a cloak of crude oil,
He knew the apprenticeship was over. In this way,
He learned about poems. He just fled to keep his hands.

Julian Stannard   *Ciao Capo*

Don't ask me if they're fake
and don't say, Will you be here tomorrow?
because I might be dead tomorrow
and how very silly to imagine
that I would have a shirt which fits.
You look bad in it Mister because you're fat
Try not eating for a week or so,
try living in Senegal for a year or two.
Try saying *Ciao capo, ciao capo, ciao capo.*
Try saying I'll have some towels next time
what colour do you like?
Try carrying these bags along the beach all day
then try doing it tomorrow and the day after.
Try pulling out a shirt and holding it there
and try looking at a stiff white finger
which says *non non* like some crazy windscreen-wiper.
Try folding the shirt up neatly
and putting it back in the bag
and then lifting the big bags and the little bags
onto your shoulders and then going down
for the bags which have not yet been lifted
I tell you Mister time whizzes by!
Who gives a fuck about Fred Perry Perry?
Just put your hands into your wallet
and give me twenty euros or thirty euros
or better still walk to the bank machine
and get out every euro you can
and stuff them into my pockets.

David Ball   *Poets in and for Palestine*

A Palestinian boy asks his father what
the plane flying overhead is made of.
It's made of iron.
And is the moon afraid of iron?
Yes, he's afraid of iron.

Israeli settlers set fire to another olive orchard.
O billowing blue clouds of perfumed smoke!
Thousand-year-old trees and a way of life
that patiently respected their gnarled resistance.

Salt tears of exile flow over stones
fall through sand
feed the green of a hill
on top of which Mahmoud Darwish is buried.
O Palestinian people, you are at least rich in this:
that you mourned three days for a poet
that you had a poet to mourn!

Hussein Al-Barghouti, father of the boy
who asked the question about the plane,
is buried within a grove of almond trees
planted by his father in the year
of the catastrophe, 1948,
of the double catastrophe:
of a people who
chosen to be just
chose injustice.

Look for him there.
Look for the poets on the hills that are left.

Carole Satyamurti   *Bound for Glory*

The short biography of an anger starts in the black box
where some hurt, a state of grace destroyed,
scored its mark on an impressionable heart.

We move to stop and search, or the News at Ten;
the anger goes underground, hides at the margins,
the back of the crowd, crusted with insults, hate.

It's homeless, shelters where it can, longing,
searches out a bookshop, a teacher, finding itself
welcome. It sets up camp in the defining story but –

now we re-enter the black box where (we can only guess)
the anger grows muscular enough to throttle itself
and sees, at last, a funnel future opening into light.

It becomes a concentrate
buys a one-way ticket
to Russell Square
boards the 8.53
heading for
heaven.

IN OTHER PLACES

Annette Skade   *Gargoyles at St Germain l'Auxerrois*

This table, this chair, bed, carpet, Chagall print, guidebook, you, me
are lines drawn in black ink on vellum, the main text no-one reads.
Real life is in the margins, lined up cheek by jowl outside our window,
a rich bestiary perched on masonry, an alley span away.

I lift the catch and they pour in, springing from corbel and dripstone,
the squat dog with the head of a fish, the baboon-faced dwarf
legs wrenched to fit the capstone, the long-haired madwoman
tortured mouth agape, spewing nothing.

Each morning when we leave I cannot shake them.
They wrap stone arms around my neck, whisper and plead,
scamper round my legs. In the evening they shuffle up
and beg me for alms. I drink them in with my wine.

They compel me to sleep in jumpers, leave windows open wide.
You shiver too – to please me, but you are hard to gull.
Now you lean elbows on the window rail, crane out from the room,
blow cigarette smoke into their very faces.

They strain towards you like the eager slaves they are,
the mouth-pullers, monsters, chimeras and grotesques.
These works of long dead labour, made lepers by time,
kiss the air by your cheek – once, twice, like Parisians do.

Anne O'Connor — *Breakfast Buffet*

The New Yorker with the clavicles says
how good her egg-white omelette tastes.
Listen, sustenance tastes more like Pan Bagnat:
cut French rolls in half, rub with garlic,
spread with olives, red pimentos, tomatoes
hearts of artichoke, pour over olive oil,
red wine vinegar, join the halves together,
rest under a heavy weight.
Eat.
So delicious it will plant
a measure of happiness, so that even
the most sorrowful heart, broken
by slammed doors and silences,
will open, open.

Pat Jourdan   *Place du Tertre*

We sit on the kerb and talk
while lights switch on in the cafés.
The easels are squatting
like sharp spiders among the cobblestones.
Around the square the tourists go
like people in a nursery rhyme
or like the nuns at dinnertime
who walk around the convent grounds
in groups of three or five
but never more
and go twice round
and then go in.

How grey the cobblestones are here
        'I have sold a painting today'
The waitresses look tired and cross
        'Perhaps the Americans will come tomorrow'
When it rains they take away the umbrellas.
        'He says he would like to see my work'
Diners are hidden at their tables among potted trees
        'They say I copy their style'
I can hear an Italian talking
        'In Holland my father is a painter'
I have decided, but I do not know what it is
        'A famous painter, yes, a famous painter'
We need some wine, red and white
        'If he saw what I was doing he would cut my throat'
I run through a Utrillo barefoot to fetch wine.

Frances Thompson   *Woodpigeons in France*

Our parlance
soft pulses of woodwind,

our notes are nouns
honed to a euphony,

a gentle hullabaloo,
our declensions.

Only our inflexions waver,
how we colour our tones

our crooning
ending, always, in this verbless question

that lilts, unanswered,
again and again through the still afternoon,

our small, baffled cadences ebbing
too soon.

David Trame　　　*The Boat from Venice*

You get off and it leaves.
Alone you listen to the moorings
whining while they resettle
after the wave.
Then, calm. The still mirror
of water by your feet and
the island.
A stretch of ochre and green.
Tiny gusts of breeze, ribbons of clouds
and the vast loitering of gulls.
Time-span.

Here you'll depend
on its regular arrival.
It will be like the tides, like breathing.
Irises crossed by rustling sunlight and waves
You'll be holding on to
an engine drone like a rising glow
on the horizon, when the prow
will appear from behind the headland,
the bow the point of an arrow
cutting into the mirror's stillness
underlining simple timelessness.

It's not only goods it will dispatch.

RELIGION

Fred Johnston   *A Beautiful Huguenot Girl Explains*
the Tree of Liberty

Its branches opened like an umbrella,
You saw that and felt safe –
When the dragoons came to Catholicise you,
They wouldn't know the sign in the trees.

Under marsh skies, a summery cold,
She opens her hands and history flies out:
A girl in flat shoes, wrapping her arms
Around herself in a wet Poitevin wind.

She knows all there is to know,
You hear the hooves chip
On the stone street, uphill, to slaughter:
You tip her, just to look at her face.

The church door frames her in a photo:
Later, you can't find the place on the map.
She hands you a ticket for another time:
Come again, she says: *The next tour's free.*

On the information desk, assorted maps,
Leaflets; the solitude is tidy, ordered –
Two dull green hills fumble upwards,
Bare as bone. You drive in the past tense.

Micocoulier tree

Andrea Porter   *Miss Taylor Experiences Jerusalem Syndrome*

I have sent the Wailing Wall to Mrs Payne.
Yesterday I wandered with the tour group
as they snapped, swam like a heat haze
before holy sights. They clung to bum bags,
life belts of passports, travellers cheques.

I was drawn to the old rituals of the Wall,
the rocking, the forehead touch, the kiss.
An American scrubbed with wet wipes
before the act. Tiny scrolls of prayers
filled every crack as flimsy mortar.

I flattened my breasts to the stone, lips
brushing the grain, caressing the scars.
I tasted the sour dust of bulldozed homes,
petrol fumes of a rush hour bus, seconds
before it was torn like an old school atlas.

I pushed my tongue deep into the open
mouth of fissures. The tip reached the salt
flavour of tears. Deeper in, settlements
with gods, tube maps, blue prints of bunkers
exploded, fizzed like bitten sherbet lemons.

I explored each crevice, found meaty truths
snagged between the wisdom teeth of Pilate.
I gagged on incense, the thick sugar coat
of words. Licking the stamp for a postcard,
I left the Wall in the gum, posted it home.

Roderick Ford   *The Dinner Guest*

Among the woodlands and green meadows
there are hints of paradise; the weave of roads
I walk upon, the rivers glinting in the sun.
The reeds whisper which way I should go
and flies rest high up in the trees and sing.

But sometimes I have other work to do,
as when I'm hurried to a home
where an old man lies among the candles,
his puffy soul still closed inside his corpse,
like a mindless face floating on the dark.

They seat me at a laden table and bid me eat
dishes that reek of cost and opulence,
thick with the fatty gravies of the dead one's sins:
I suck away layers of softest skin like masks,
I swallow the disguises of his soul.

When I'm tight with wickedness they shove me out,
as though any dog could take on sins unscathed.
But I walk the briars and wildways for a day,
until I find a scarecrow in some lonely field
and just beneath its rangy arse I shit

the plump and steaming coil of that man's sins.
I watch sweet flies descend to lay their eggs,
knowing maggots soon will bathe and suckle there.
When I'm long gone those grubs will turn to flies
and sins will rise like prayers upon the winds.

With heaven in my eyes I walk these roads
and though I'm shunned none will do me harm,
for they all must take the sacrament of death,
that sustains me like the soft preserving hand
of my Lord who is the voice among the reeds.

James Harpur   *St Patrick's Return*

I sensed at once the yearning for release.
March mists dispelled the coloured countryside
And hung in curdled webs from ragged trees.

Soft rain soaked fields of stationary bulls
Where gangs of crows were cackling like the druids
Who came to curse me, clacking jaws of skulls.

I heard the people crying out in sin;
The eyes of severed heads still globed their hell
Of rats and fire, blood and drink.

My prayers were sucked from me and overnight
God's love descended like a snowfall.
The blackthorns opened up their petalled light

And everywhere I tapped my staff, my wand,
The fields and trees leaped up and greened the land.

Susan Connolly   *The Deer's Cry*

*Patrick said this after King Laoghaire
set out from Tara to kill him.*

I have lit the holy fire
and you are angry,
but I am peaceful
as the white deer grazing
in the woods at Slane.
  Brightness of sun
    whiteness of snow
      splendour of fire
We do not know each other
but we will meet soon.
We are like two hills
on either side of the river.
  Speed of lightning
    sea-depth
      firmness of rock
Some may go in chariots,
and some on horses,
but I walk in the name
                of my God.
  God's wisdom guide me
    God's word speak for me
      God's path before me
Your chariots cross the Boyne;
you want to destroy
the living fire.
                I sing:
Christ where I lie
  Christ where I sit
    Christ where I rise
              I sing
  Christ in every eye that sees me
  Christ in every ear that hears me.

Who makes you think
that I and my monks
are eight wild deer
entering the woods at Slane
with the fawn, Benen, following?

Jeanette McCullough

230

John O'Leary   *Columba and Easter*

One day telleth another, and one night certifieth another – Psalm 19

The dispute between Columba and the Pope in Rome over the true date of Easter drew an equator across the world.

The Pope wished to impose a calculus so that all of the known world would worship together, but Columba would not agree on the day, because for Columba it was always Easter, and God was always dead:

> For this is how
> we live inside
> the world – not know-
> ing if he'll rise.

Archbishop Arculf came from the south, blown by a storm of wind, with an offering for Columba from the Pope Gregory, to persuade him.

It was a box containing, he said, a sliver of the true cross. Columba opened the reliquary and it was empty, but he had it placed on the high altar on Iona nonetheless, in honour of the pontiff, and because, as he said, it really did contain a fragment of the true cross:

> For what do we know
> except despair?
> God is the No-
> thing that is there.

The debate over the correct date of Easter
was really one about the independence
of the Celtic church. It was resolved at the
Synod of Whitby (663 A.D.)
after a century of dispute

Paul Maddern   *Lines at Lacken Mill*

for Vita

> *How lovely it is today!*
> *The sunlight breaks and flickers*
> *On the margin of my book.*
> Ninth Century Irish monastic gloss, anonymous.

The shower has passed but rain drops
from the canopy to play the river like a drum,
and I'm absorbed by the performance
of a wayward beat falling on the page.
The *a* in apple blossoms and the *b*
in beauty blooms, infecting with the bleed
all well meaning words.
            And just as well.

For I would tell you limply
that the mill cat rests beside me, the dog
transfixed by swans. And I would write
of an ancient weir, broking for a race
of herds pastured for millennia
slurping waters that the friendless heron scours;
of the river's remorseless measure
over worn, familial rocks
and of eddies they maintain for their devoted salmon.
I might even reach and reference linnet's wings.
But you have heard all this, and are immune.

Perhaps a fashion's passed –
as these spots, in time, diminish.
Still, I'll take some pleasure
from a perfect finish:
a single-note magnificat,
the climax to the great tympanic act,
falls, then fades in a quickening river.

And now the page is parched. Old *a's* and *b's*
that advocated venture have been stemmed.
But you, attuned to perfect labours, know
dried blooms and blossoms will be shamed
when, shortly, we will witness birth again.

Philip Quirke   *Straw*

(December 6, 1273)

A dry-stone outhouse looks towards mountains.
Empty except for a rusty plough
and a square bale of straw from some distant harvest.

Chinks in the walls, fractures in the corrugated roof
admit slivers of sun or moon, but high-summer light
pierces through to dim corners: then

the straw blazes like polished bronze,
like thatch aflame, like sparks from an earth fissure.
It radiates a sheen like a burning bush.

Shadows and silence descend as the earth turns.
The bale reverts to a musty heap of damp,
useless as fodder, forgotten, abandoned.

*

Aquinas, midway through the *Summa*,
saw his tryst with Mystery as straw:
Thereafter, he spoke and wrote no more.

Leanne O'Sullivan　　　*Children of the Cillíneach*

Come to us with lilies and meadowsweet,
come to us by heart and not by sight,
that heaving of love which aches still,
coffined in your belly's darkening loam.

Mother, I've known your weight
and the length of your soft hands
bent over this rugged, unworked soil.
I've known you by the forgetful daisies

strung with blue and red twine.
I open my eyes. You are watching me.
If ever I am allowed a voice
you will know me when I speak:

whatever is unwinged in nothingness
comes home with a memory of wings.
That scythe which undercuts life I remember,
and, above, birdsong, the petals

of daisies settling. I tell you,
I will know you again among the crickets
and billowing trees. We will survive the earth.
Are you not my mother?

Was it not you I heard in the thrashing dark?
The one whose hands
I felt unbury me and baptise my soul
in a fountaining of tears?

Cillíneach: a burial place for infants who died before baptism

Seán Hewitt   *The Moor*

Is this the man that came from Dublin to start
The dig? His bones, light like cuttlefish, shiver
In the wind; lamb-tongued lover of the land.

They say this boulder was plucked like an egg
From the mouth of the road, which led the cars
Away from the site where the old life slept

Like numbers under scratchcard silver.
Someone scraped up jointed writhes of rock
And found a thing they used to dry the hay,

A graveyard, a stone cross marked *Domine*.
I've heard he stepped down into the pit
And anchored himself there, sought out the

Marbled roots of furze and wedged his feet
Beneath them. There, the eager air chorded him
To the bow of its tongue, and played him

Until his body's hollow sang the song
Of the godless children that lay at his feet:
The roots fixed, and limbo lowed through his ribs
Till he swelled on the moor like a moon.

Eva Bourke   *Achill Killeen*

1.

Early morning.
The holiday cottages across the bay are tired
from rowing all night through the surf
and lay their oars aside.

Far out between two rocks the sun opens
a blue door and ushers a trawler and crew
into the glittering high rise of the day.

2.

A tortoiseshell butterfly leads me
to where the waves unravel
all over the sand.
It is a scrap of the lost map
of the island blown here and there
with its brown wings
and delicate black delineations.

3.

I stand in a field above the sea strewn with pieces
of white quartz
each marking a child's grave.

The stones are bright lamps lifted
out from the earth and placed
on a makeshift altar:

the old gods have come down
from the mountains
to watch over the field in pity and silence.

4.

The children had slipped out of reach
and into the earth so fast
their names were not written on stone.

But the young parents who knelt
on the hillside knew them by heart –
grief they were called, *loss* and *anguish*.

5.

All day a mild wind rakes the grass
and the clouds rush their cargo
of birds eastwards.
All day my feet go
here and there – all day my heart
wants to stand still.

A killeen was a graveyard for children who died unbaptised.

John Montague   *Scraping the Pot*

I knelt by my bedside every night
To beg forgiveness for every petty act
Against life, beating the dog,
Or, more seriously, striking some
Senior being across the arm
In the throes of a tantrum,
Like my old aunt, bony and sweet,
(that memory can still hurt)
And never doubted once
That from some azure heaven
A merciful Christ looked down.

His face loomed nearest
When I crossed the aisles
Of our cold chapel in Garvaghey
To kneel in line for Confession.
(It began when I was seven,
And had reached the Age of Reason.)
The grille sliding, the probing whisper,
The halting story to that bowed shadow.
Finally, the Act of Contrition,
That strange lightheadedness
Of release, after the Blessing.

Scraping the pot, the country
People called it, and
I saw my neighbours' souls
Hanging above the hearth,
Scoured and gleaming.

Gréagór Ó Dúill   *Hare's Ears and Complicity*

I concern myself with the high translucent ears
    of the young hare in the field beside my window
    now the sheep have gone, the grass grows young.

I consider the local usage of the dative of possession
    and the plural of respect they give here to the priest
    as the language ebbs like the sea on the great strand, leaving pools.

My friend stands at the window of the school, his hands behind his back,
    watches the boats to the islands, the slow erosion of the sandhills
    turns and asks the children for the answer to the sums.

The priest came here this morning, we discussed
    his several poems, memoir pieces, sentiment and language.
    I nearly promised to help find a publisher, he drove on then to the school.

Another teacher stands at the next window,
    a nine-year-old sitting on the deep sill beside him, trying not to cry
    as master fondles his silken penis
    (Cavafy's adjective, if I remember right)
    and the class breathes shallow, heads down, eyes flickering.

A mother tells the priest, as she tells all,
    in boxed whispers through a grille:
    is told no child brings this on self but one so taught at home,
    none persisting in such scandal-mongering
    stays where they were raised.

I hear the cuckoo back, now pipits nest
    and watch the arc of swallows, after flies,
    I draft my pastorals, attend the season's change,
    the light through ears of a maturing hare, my small cathedral windows.

Owen Gallagher   *FishR4U*

In 2011, the Catholic Bishops of England and Wales
re-established the eating of fish on Fridays.

Perhaps the saint responsible for penances
            won the toss with God: once again
            worshippers can queue outside
            'Only Codding' for the flesh of fish,
            eased down with salt 'n' vinegar
            and blessed at the family table with Ketchup.

I suspect the Bishops' earthly advisers
            are unaware of increasingly fishless seas
            and have not hooked up with the fish gods
            in Brussels, captains in suits
            determined to restock our waters,
            who have prescribed laws like Moses,
            sunk more boats than Drake,
            and forced trawler-men to beach
            their boats on e-bay.

Perhaps a miracle will occur and parishioners
            can queue on Fridays at church
            to receive a sliver of fish.

I offer these thoughts in the name of the Cod, the Plaice, the Haddock.

Noel Monahan   *Black Madonna of Nessebar*

She is pearl of the Black Sea, shrouded
In frescoes, embedded in sweet smelling incense,
Alight with innumerable candles. She has been
Sentenced to silence for long periods, times when God
Was scarce on the ground. She is dark, her face
Has roots in the sun, flames from the stake still
Colour her complexion. I recognise her
In the faces of old women, eyes shut,
Lips feeding on prayer. I hear her in the rhymes
Of school children, in the chatter of seagulls
From the rooftops. She is one with the pictures
Of the dead left hanging on doors, walls, trees ...
At one with the strings of salt fish drying in the wind.
Every cobbled street leads to her and the sea.

Angela France   *For a Young Priest*

                    so you've learned that a shadow
is not always just a shadow   and that yours
        will burn at your heels   darken the edge
of your sight   from now on

        and you've found
that margins lie   ruler straight
on the page   but shift   slippery
under your feet   when you walk them

what you expected   is nothing but
            scribbles on paper
what you know   dissolves in daylight
leaves only ash

you thought keeping clean
    was simple   now you know
what you touch
                leaves a stain

Edward Denniston   *To the Bishop My Brother*

No, I do not feel blue, as you say, or the least humble,
or indeed less wise when I sit on a sultry night
as you suggest, in my garden, gazing at the stars,
or imagining the vast, weighty, noiseless space
between them; nor, when I take time to stop
and stare at the bulk of the mountain, or down
from the cliff-top to the churning sea do I feel
the least bit small or insignificant as you imagine
I should. Although the line from the Japanese poet
vast landscapes bring men to a halt has
an authoritative ring, to me its sonorous tone
means nothing. I do not think or feel it is God
diminishing me to the smallness of a child,
that I might see and know his vastness, his hugeness,
like Milton's giant, slumbering in the sea,
posing as salvation's island. But I do know
something much greater than myself —
a man who tends his dying mother everyday,
emptying her bedpan, reading her towards sleep
with Christina Rossetti, stroking her forehead
so she'll know, up to the end, what touch is for
as he listens for words of sense when her eyes
eagerly look up in search of a son. Thinking about
this man, I look up too and lean back, straining to see
something insurmountable, something beyond me. Then I am
as you say, dear brother, *diminished*, and simply *here*,
placed in a scale of things I hardly understand.

Derek Coyle   *That City*

(after Jaroslav Seifert, for Pope Benedict XVI)

That city had grown fat with developers,
land grabbers and sellers, her arteries
clogged with solicitors, engineers, useless
actors, singers, artists. Her churchmen
a cancer on once tender skin, having forgotten
God's love for the frailest human being.
God raged at what he saw: Georgian streets
choked with corruption, moral ineptitude
and turpitude on every corner, such that
his mouth foamed. He stormed through
the rooms of heaven shouting:
'what black sinners! Torrents of sulphur,
thunderstorms of fire should blast them
a hundred and twenty days.' He drew
breath, held back, reached deep into his heart
recalling a promise made long ago:
for two righteous men, two decent folk,
he'd spare that city. He looked down
and saw two men, lovers
for many years, leaving a night club
having danced to their heart's content:
the night's tenderness lay before them,
its eternity of erotic bliss and sweet nothings.
God blinked as his eye brightened, how could he
deny them this, a tear trailed his cheek
as he saw hope in these angels.

Penelope Shuttle   *Quakers' House at Come-to-Good*

Unadorned interior
Bare boards, kitchen chairs,
everything else dispensed-with

No urgencies of art or plot
Thought lives here
alone with thought

Outside, the garden's adorned,
chockful of primroses,

yellow piety and exuberance
that also had faith in silence,
does not waste words

Penelope Shuttle   *Silence Had Forgotten*

Silence had forgotten
ever wanting to be among the spoken

Silence was newmade, opaque,
more singular than any opera

It was also
what nobody in the world wanted

Silence was something else,
the other side of itself,

a caress
ferociously praising

a bridge it used to possess

Valeria Melchioretto   *Rodinsky's Room*

Rumours have it he was a scholar of esoteric insights,
others called him a golem in a garret, the last meshuga
in the neighbourhood, a cabalist with see-through skin
like a shop-window where sadness was for sale.

His home was a hothouse of secrets. The staircase sagged
like an invalid's broken spine. All inhabitants held on
to balustrade and dogma. The synagogue was in the vault
while the attic, far from heaven, was filled with upheaval.

Then he vanished without A-Z and not down Brick Lane
for a pint of milk. Some say, a mummified cat was found
next to an imprint of his head on the bed and something grey
as brain sat in a porridge bowl, prove he cracked the script.

Scrolls had been food-for-thought and turned into cocoons
as he rolled in erudition like a bobbin among the bobbins
belonging to Huguenot silk-weavers, the previous tenants.
The mystic or fool glimpsed God in thin air and joined him.

Or did the script crack him, haunted by the gutter's gossip?
The stench of insult and snobbery was driving the residents
around the stair's bends which never lead to a higher plane.
But one by one they went insane, wherever that might be.

John F. Deane   *Reasons of the Heart*

for Paddy Bushe

Reason dictates one does not build a monastery
          on a desolate high rock miles out to sea; reason
          knows it as a soaring-place for fulmar, a burrow-home
          for the tubenose shearwater; and yet –

should you stand, one night, when the sea
          breathes quietly below, when the sky has grown
          close and spectacular in its stars, should you watch
          this day's companion rise, crisscross upwards through the dark

with only the shifting light of his storm-lantern telling
          his passageway to the heavens – then you will know
          you are safe here, out of the world's wildering. The soul
          thrives in compulsive prayers and praisings;

so climb, pilgrim, to heights that take the breath away
          until you stand at last, head in the clouds, undaunted;
          to carve, over years-or-life, rough cruciform shapes
          out of the livid rock may be a poem to what reason calls

foolishness: word made stone, made bone, clay-floor
          and weathers. Here you may miss the galloping of horses
          over sward, but you are rid of newspapers, banks
          and metaphysical concerns. Perhaps, who knows? the Christ

shifts stealthily about the slopes, freed from reason's grounds,
          here where seals come, heaving themselves onto rock
          to flop and doze, their deep-voiced moaning songs
          calling out crazed praise to their Creator.

Sam Gardiner   *How It Will Be*

A shadow slipping along the street,
a thought passing, someone returning
to tell you that while life was a great idea
death is a better. Or they have come back
from a wordless place to tell us about it,
but not in words. This is how it will be.
A Neanderthal gardener came weekly,
no one knew from where. His scalp
reached his eyebrows and obviated the need
for forehead. Through time he was here
no more. The gardens miss him,
but sometimes the neighbours see him
weeding their leeks by moonlight,
which is super-natural to the present day's
primitive sub-naturalists. This will be
natural in times to come, for ghosts exist
as soon as someone sees them. Normality
was when Mum, now a ghost, was getting
ready to water the garden and God said
'Allow Me' and she would put the watering
can back in the shed. How great they wert,
those fully clothed short-lived creatures
who gathered to raise their voices in praise
of a greater than they, temps praying for
permanent positions. This is how it will be.
The young woman in dark light-patched green
who has wandered Bradley Woods for centuries
calling for her stolen child will deny
that ghostliness is the last stage of reality,
that missing children become imaginary
as time passes. In truth they become more
real than we are. This is how it will be.

Nick Bridson Baker   *Icarus Stein or Kleine*

His name may have been Stein or Kleine
A Jewish tailor from Rue Lacharrière or Lachelier
Who wanted to fly so much he stitched together two big wings of feathers

Men crossed the Channel in balloons before the French Revolution
But man's first flight was still to come when
Stein or Kleine got onto a chair above the parapet at the top of the Eiffel Tower

A movie camera was present but sound was not
So we have it all in black and white and silence
As the camera turns, Stein or Kleine spreads his large feathered wings

Looks towards the ground, makes as if to go but seems unsure
And lowers his outstretched arms. The scene is hard to watch
Is the man beside him in the hat asking him to, for God's sake, reconsider ?

They speak. Stein or Kleine opens his wings again, pauses then
Puts one foot on the parapet and steps over the edge.
He drops out of sight at the bottom of the screen.

Now to his delight his wings hold, unseen by the camera
He turns in a big glide over Paris
Stein or Kleine is flying.

Martin Dyar   *Divinity and Hare*

I stayed with her because she seemed unwell.
You could wait, I said, and choose another form,
some other creature, another time or means.
You needn't send yourself into this change.
But though she was a being full of doubt,
there at the stream, at the field's edge, she stood
and made her mind a door to the heart of the hare.
And then, as gods in this mode sometimes do,
she conjured for herself a kind of breath
and spat divine reluctance to the ground.
And summer seemed to take this as a cue:
the field smells were a sunlit channel now
and walls of birds eclipsed my last advice
to her, timid, transformed, hell bent on life.

Maureen Jivani   *Lessons for Cubs*

...in the distant past, humans and animals were
not as clearly distinguished as they are today.
– Encyclopaedia of World Myths

Remember a skinned bear may look like man.
Never take off your coat in company.

We are not only hunters but hunted.
Wherever possible cover your tracks.

Do not be caught out at small talk, or debating.
The philosophy of consciousness is a trap.

Growls will strengthen the oppressor's axe.
Keep this in mind. Even as parading on two legs

gains us height our noses will be further
                    from the ground.

Anne-Marie Fyfe   *White Sheets*

A stark flotilla from a Giacometti nightmare
rounds the basalt outcrop. Misses landfall
by a good sea mile.

At Ocean House the residents who've long
abandoned sleep, stand gumboot-deep
in rose-bed mulch at the low shrubbery wall
or lurch forward out of bath chairs to gaze
mesmerised through the sun-parlour's condensation,
mark the spectre fleet's passing,
ensure the swell's amplitude
recedes to normal.
                    In Tuesday's
sub-post-office they deny they ever saw a thing
but they can't lose the clatter of rigging,
the gale-howl of sheets for days. And more days.

The chief coastguard swears you could chart
the astronomical year by this apparition. Put it down
to the miasma of dreams if you like,
but how do you account for the shoal
of dead white flounder scattered round
your sea-washed and fresh-dried
front-entrance steps at daybreak.

David Andrew   *All Day, the Rain*

*'When is a culture as a whole to be thought of as a
system of modifications of our lives as talkers?
And would this imply that there is something
undefined in human life, pre-cultural as it were?'*
– Cavell

In the exquisite factory of the cell
life lives on. A language at one with
the long chemical that, some billion years
before culture, stumbled upon a story
it could retell with almost no error,
over and over again.

What was this story, 'pre-cultural' as it were?
The business of staying in business.
Thus, the snail, beautiful in the mowed grass,
does not know its shell tells an exquisite story.
A smallest whorl, its earliest it, carried about
on its back like the rings in a tree,
an autobiography.

In the end was the word: telling how, *making*
our supposes true. All day, the rain falls
down from the great sky, the light hammering
down on this conservatory roof, knocking
on the windows. This snail is in his house,
shut up tight with his foot on the wall
till his time comes – and not a word about him.

Consider the branches of the birch
how they bend. Consider the peonies –
their flowers dressed as if for a ball, as if
to attend on a Queen, drenched and humble.
A very long time before we come to a man
who, mulling over 'forms of life', asks a large
question: What *is* going on?

253

Leontia Flynn   *Bobby Fischer (1943-2008)*

After the 1972 24-game match in Reykjavik,
Fischer 'didn't play any of the great tournaments,
and refused lucrative offers to endorse products
saying he couldn't because he didn't use them'.
                                    – Wikipedia

Endgame – the King is toppled. Bobby Fischer,
whose cold war bout in coldest Reykjavik
gripped the split world, has died. The game is over –
Rook, Pawns, Bishop plays Knight, Pawns and Rook
Checkmate.
          High-octane mother: check. *Strain*: check.
(When begged to play by arch-fiend Kissinger
The Soviets suspected dirty tricks:
'please check the light fittings, yes? ; check the radiator'.)
Then exile and paranoia: check – I'd take
The snow-cold path to ancient Thingvellir
And trace his short biog there in white and black –
from Brooklyn – to beard, baths ... and kidney failure
through squares solved and unsolved – to understand
The games – these moves – that fix the fitful mind.

Luis Fanti

254

Karen O'Connor   *Someone Let the Fire Go Out*

and darkness walked freely
in and out as if it owned our lives.
And we searched for a glint of something,
a spark to show a path along a gravel bed
with wild flowers growing at angles
and hoof prints to navigate through.

But our ember died as quickly as it pierced the dark
and flared our irises and lost us the subtleties
of the night, only leaving the black empty voice,
someone let the fire go out.

And we found ourselves stumbling in the cold
only seeing what our minds remembered,
that ghostly image of negative space,
caught there between two worlds
and still we believed the path was there,
though we couldn't see it,
could no longer feel it, or smell it, or sense it,
but we believed,
and in the path lies the answer –
which is no longer important –
only to know how to light the fire
before it's too late.

Ivy Bannister   *Pellet*

Silver talons. Fiery pulse of wings.
Out of the night sky Mother plummets,
breaks the neck with a blow.

The air stinks of Chanel and blood.
She rips the carcass, tidily
wolfs entrails.

Sated eyes gleam. She preens
her barbs and barbules
with a burgundy beak, puffs up

then floats into the sky,
the heels of her stilettos
speckled with diamonds,

the stars her oyster, the beat
of great furred wings leisurely now
as she soars over city and countryside.

At dawn her gorge casts the indigestibles:
bone fused with tooth, hair,
a heart-shaped locket.

John Wakeman   *The Ideal City*

On the first evening, having rested,
he called us to him and asked for a city –
described it for us, word upon word,
so that it rose in the firelight
like a giant jewel, shining above the huts
from the river to the forest edge.

Lives and years were lost,
levering the white stones from the mountain
to the river bank.
The architect never faltered,
spending his fierce strength against the sullen rock,
raising the fallen, forgiving the dying,
teaching us what little we could learn.

White mansions we built for the poor
along the bright boulevards,
a theatre for the festivals of drumming,
a library to house the yellow skin
on which our filthy history was scratched.

And in the centre of it all we raised,
taller than trees,
the tomb of marble where our leader lies,
just at the place where he was sacrificed.

We go there even now,
after so long,
leaving our huts to marvel
at those crumbling towers,
mildewed frescoes, grass-grown avenues,
and go home full of pride at what we wrought.

Doireann Ní Ghríofa   *In the Museum of Missing Things*

I am the custodian of this exhibition of erasures. I am curator of loss.
I watch over pages and pages of scribbles, deletions, obliterations
in a museum that protects not what is left, but what is not.

Where arteries runs free, I hold the homeless clots
I collect all the lasered tattoos that let flesh start again.
In this exhibition of erasures, I am curator of loss.

See the unravelled wool that was once a soldier's socks
shredded documents, the kink of untied knot in shoestrings –
my museum protects not what is left, but what is not.

I keep millions of jpegs of strangers caught with their eyes crossed,
and the circle of pale skin where you removed your wedding ring.
I recall all the names you ever forgot. I am curator of loss.

Here, the forgotten need for the flint & steel of a tinderbox.
In corners I store barbers' piles of hair, ash, wiped fingerprints.
I protect not what is left, but what is not.

I keep shrapnel pulled from wounds where children were shot,
confession sins, abortions, wildflowers smothered in cement.
I am the custodian of this exhibition of erasures. I am curator of loss
in this museum that protects not what is left, but what is not.

WORDS

Anthony Thwaite   *Accismus*

When we speak
We mean more than we say.
Words do not go away.
Whatever dumb compulsions urge us on
We are too weak
To damp them down.
Accismus is our way:
'A feigned refusal of what is most desired.'
The will is tired,
Gives in too easily, lies there
Pretending not to care
Whatever's thrown away and burned,
And nothing left except this smoky air
As if it happened when my back was turned.

Alex Barr   *Misunderstandings . . .*

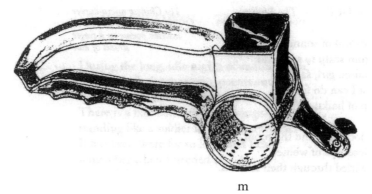

m
i
s
u
n
d
e
r
s
t
a
n
d
i
n
g
s
and
uncertainties arise
when I mince my words

Conor McCarthy   *Paper Post*

for Deirdre

Sending a packet of papers, folded up,
across land and sea
seems a doubty way to talk now
in the days that are in it.
These are days of haste.
Electric letters clattering from satellite to satellite.
But this paper's slowness
is some small measure of the span of the world;
of the space between
the smell of eucalyptus and the Pacific,
red soil, blue sky,
and the taste of bog peat and salt rain,
slate clouds, and soft Atlantic mists.

According to Terence Dolan's Dictionary of Hiberno-English,
*'the days that are in it' would mean 'the days we are talking
about at present' – these days.*

Maggie Butt   *Heathrow? Heathrow?*

Sometimes the contours of a stranger's face
imprint themselves, as though they map my life
or reveal coordinates of wider mysteries.
My tube pulls in to Leicester Square and through the glass
I watch a silent film: a Rabbi on the packed platform
invisible to everyone but me, holds up a scrap of paper,
chants his English mantra *Heathrow? Heathrow?*
as though invoking the secret names of God.
People surge round him like a tide. He a pebble,
buffetted on the beach, irrelevant to the hugeness of the ocean.
This isn't prejudice. This is its guilty twin, indifference.
He, lonelier than a man left in a desert,
knowing his insignificance under the sweeping span of stars.
He is beyond my reach, beyond the carriage-glass
his battered suitcase at his feet, his hat, his curls,
his wiry beard, the paper talisman which he, a scholar,
had relied on. Words are his trade, his sanctuary, as mine.
Heathrow? Heathrow? the prayer
of waves upon a shore.

John Mole   *Acceptance Speech at the Oscars*

thank you thank you all of you so much
you can't begin to know not in the world
not in a month of Sundays what does that mean
why did I say that my grandmother used to say it
if only she could see me up here standing here
wow if I'd have ever thought no really
I'd have written something down oh my god
no absolutely not no never this is for all of you
wait let me catch my breath wait
no sorry sorry this isn't the real me no really
I'm not like this not if you knew me
anyone will tell you let me tell you
what I've just thought about this little girl
not me not me her first audition
they told her what the story was she has to cry
because her mother dies wait this is true
I have to tell you it's so cute and so professional
you'll understand you've been there
all of you it's why you're here they told her
look away back up to camera then straight ahead
and think of anything that made her sad
until the tears arrived but they were there already
all she had to ask was this one question
how do you want them all the way
or half way down my face o god
that's acting though not me not now
these tears I don't know where they are
all over the place control yourself
I must look awful in this light but all of you
you're beautiful pure gold and every one of you
is why I'm here so thank you thank you
what more to say I'd say it if I could
if I'd written something down that little girl
it wasn't me I love you all you'll never know
how much you've given me how much I owe
to the little tricks they teach us at the studio

Gabriel Rosenstock   *Focal*

Focal atá acu in Tierra del Fuego:
Mamihlapinatapai
Féachaint ar a chéile, an gníomh sin,
Ag súil go ndéanfaidh
Páirtí éigin díobh
Rud éigin atá inmhianaithe
(Dar leis an dá pháirtí)
Ach nach bhfuil fonn rómhór
Ar cheachtar den dá pháirtí
A dhéanamh.

Gabriel Rosenstock   *A Word*

A word they have in Tierra del Fuego:
Mamihlapinatapai –
The act of looking at each other
Hoping that one of the parties concerned
Will carry out some desirable deed
(Desired by both parties)
But which neither party
Is much in the mood
To carry out.

WRITING

Gerry Murphy   *Night and the Muse*

after Juan de la Cruz

On a moonless night in a flare of longing
I slipped out unnoticed,
my empty house unaware.

Disguised by utter darkness,
I descended by a secret ladder
into the silent yard and climbed out into the fields.

Guided by an inner light
that blazed without betraying a gleam of illumination,
I passed in shadow.

And there, alone by the river,
your hair caressed by stray night breezes,
I found you.

Laying your head on my shoulder,
your gentle touch overwhelmed me
and I lost track of my senses.

I came to, leaning against you,
my cares set aside,
forgotten amongst the brambles.

for Angelique

Maitreyabandhu   *The Irish Muse*

for Bernard O'Donoghue

At Tottenham Court Road the metal shutters
had been pulled across and even after I walked
along the busy pavements up to Goodge Street
I got it wrong and had to double back.
I waited. And as I read your poems, a woman,
young and blonde and slightly drunk,
judging from her breath, asked me what I read.
We talked about the Irish Muse. She said
she came from Inniskeen, the town
where Patrick Kavanagh was born, and how
they hadn't anything better to do there
than go off somewhere in their mind.

Jeanette McCullough

266

Anna Woodford   *Desk*

Dad raised his hand, the gavel fell,
    the following week the delivery man
left no stair uncursed
    as he dragged the desk like a cross
to my room. It was stuck
    by the dressing table, catching my hip
when I danced in the mirror.
    It wasn't a dog or a TV,
it was a leg-up with the La Sagesse entrance exam,
a short step from there to university.

It was laden with trifles and pellucid jellies
when I started to write. I saw myself
crowned with leaves in the reflected glory
    of the bay that overlooked
all the fences. There was a room
    – a whole wing – of my parents' house
that they hadn't discovered. I entered
    through the desk like a wardrobe,
Mum sneaked in after me, cleaning up
    poems like snow from my floor.

Betty Thompson   *Showing*

Look, a tooth in the hand.
He wants to show it to me.
Rushes through the runners,
kickers, throwers, skippers,
shouters, screamers, chasers,
jumpers, strollers, sitters,
lone shufflers.
It just came out. Creamy and grey,
trickle of blood.
Wrap it up, pocket it.
Sleep on it later.

Look, a poem in the hand.
He wants to show it to me.
Sidles out of nowhere.
It's finished now. Creased jotter page,
lines and lines of pencil words.
Reads it out, pockets it.
Might unfold it later.

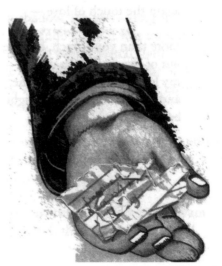

Jeanette McCullough

Saint James Harris Wood   *While None of It Is Mine*

I don't care about the underwear,
never did, the t-shirts & shorts are fine,
utilitarian, white & humorless;
the hats are generic:
cheap gray baseball caps & weary dark blue beanies
like low rent gangsters wear as uniforms & disguises;
don't mind the shoes, heavy brown work boots,
bland & surprisingly sturdy,
owned by no one in the real world
except long-standing bachelors
who wander around in swamps;
wish I had some other pants,
anything except these god damned stiff blue ones
long ago forsook by fashion,
PRISONER written up & down the right leg
in case there's an earthquake & someone escapes;
I loathe the matching shirts,
designed by artless sons of bitches
who are used to clothing mental patients
in shapeless light blue smocks with no ambition,
except to mark us as dead to the world;
I hate wearing this fucking life,
bound by careless barbed wire & lies,
nothing real;
but made to last.

I like my glasses,
they remind me ...
of lost libraries, faraway bookstores
& poetry written by my children.

Niall R. Walsh   *from A Leitrim Elegy*

in memory of John McGahern

You were among the last, John
To feel that spiritual wrath
Made flesh, sinew and bone
In alliance with secular power,
To feel the wavering harmony
Of crozier and portfolio descend
In one concordant blow.
The rusty iron school gates
Creaking furtively closed on you,
Confused fear in colleagues' averting eyes
That sent you on our national trudge
Into the slip-stream carrying thousands
By heaving ferry and rattling train
To the capital of our old refuge.
Where the altar, wiped clean of the blood
Of O'Casey, Beckett and O'Donnell
Stood ready for your reluctant form.
Editors of *Criterion* and *The Bell*,
Simmering exiles from the Censorship Board,
Stood round in priestly array,
While basting fat bubbled and spat,
Incense wafted to the lights,
The knife flashed on its block.
Another martyr for Liberal Ireland
Was sizing-up your frame.
But you turned from the bitter
Comforts of censure and propaganda,
Returning, even to where you got your wound
To live, unreproaching and unquestioning
Among the rhythms and rituals
That circle you without reproof.

Theo Dorgan   *Travelling Man*

for Michael Hartnett

Winter is nearly over,
mud frost in the gutters,
iceferns on car windscreens,
feather-buds on the willow.

Spring will be here,
spearheads of crocus,
restless teenagers,
foxes rattling bins;

and one man who would
hear and see and honour
these things will not call
or answer, or be here.

The moon is a shaving of ice, a boat
lapping him out beyond the emigrant jets.

Pat Boran   *The Princess of Sorrows*

i.m. Michael Hartnett

The Princess of Sorrows blames herself
and cannot disguise it. For too long now
she has sat on this footpath and no longer knows
the way home. In the hostel she feels
she will one day vanish, even to herself.
On a night like this only a doorway
seems solid. So five nights a week
she comes to sit here, her head to one side,
as though the fall or the blow
that has scarred her nose since yesterday
had snapped her neck. Rag-doll princess,
inner child of the inner city
set adrift, I touch your sleeve,
I drop a note in your paper cup,
I greet you in English, in Irish, in Greek,
or something that sounds like Greek; I speak
Lorca's Spanish, the Latin of Catullus,
two or three words of Romanian learned
one night in a bar from two drunken thieves
equally lost... And then it passes,
the dance within me, and I tip
the tip of my flat cap, click my heels
like poetry's Fred Astaire, and bow
low before you in inherited shame
at having so little to offer you here
where the cars flow past in a river of lights,
and we are not strangers, not any more,
but the Princess of Sorrows and Hartnett the poet,
both of us homeless in every language known.

Mary Noonan   *No Direction Home*

in memory of Gregory O'Donoghue

I wrote that the final days of August would find me
washed up, propped in a place where the light of day
is tight and mean. You approved, gently tending –
even laments for summer were safe with you,
lines too concerned with the small ambit of seasons
to encompass the impact of a true ending.

And so it was that August swept you off your feet,
quenched your breath with ease as she dragged
hurricanes and swollen waters in her train.
In the middle of your fifty-fourth year –
one of the bald facts mourners swapped at the grave,
suddenly aware that they knew you not at all.

I knew only the grace of your yellowed fingers,
that elegant pen, your hand feathering its tender script
across a page, your hooded eyes, your mug of gin,
the small room where we met once a week.
I saw you sometimes, walking lopsidedly in the street;
once, at a launch, we talked about Bob Dylan

but in the moment I heard of your death I knew
that you had guided me to a place – a room, a page –
where limping and stammering come into their own,
a vast, airy space inviting me to stand my ground,
to bellow in tantrum, to rampage, to thrive
in my brokenness.

Aidan Hayes   *I Want, I Want . . .*

after Hugh Mac Diarmid (1892-1978)

     poems like guitars that kill fascists
Poems persistent as the sea
     powerful as Quasimodo
Poems like wild poppies in Donegal ground
     pungent as a sudden greenfinch
Poems that censor nothing human
     that sing like Paul Robeson
They singe the page
Poems like mackerel that straighten fish hooks
They catch the curt sound of carwheels through puddles
Poems dynamic with Yeatsian rage
These poems give the news due attention
Poems that show lobelias' exact blue
Unafraid of farting of yelling of rude red health
Poems that detest the word untouchable
They scale the walls round the cabbage patch of the heart
Poems with opened mouth and ears and eyes and pores
Poems sharp-beaked with questions
     spiked with exclamations invisibly inked
Poems that challenge a *minority* pursuit
These are not nourished by wine and politeness
They are poems both crafted and crafty
Poems that take you by the lapels and shake
Poems that speak the word poor the word rich
Poems that serve neither master nor mistress
These poems worship the god of Life
Unfazed by Power
     they embrace human being
Poems not collared and tied
Like crowds of starlings they make the air shimmer
Poems with strong arms outstretched
Poems with fists and with hands
Poems that fight with the Self

Clare Sawtell   *Poems on Ash Wednesday*

i.m. Seamus Heaney

The place was full, we nearly didn't make it,
a string of us were let in at the back.

He arrived without fuss, black briefcase straps hanging loose
and began with the wind, how if he'd been asleep he would have
missed it and from then on we were all eyes and ears.

It was about simple things – folding sheets, a fountain pen, and then
the words held up something and other scenes flashed past:
the box kite that caught me on the ear, collecting windfalls, it was
all there, nothing grand, words brushing worlds,
another sacramental.

Luis Fanti

275

Dolores Stewart   *Aftermath*

Walter of the beads and rosaries, Aodh mac Aingil
of the scholar's slate, Tadhg Gaelach of the ha'penny songs –
All famished. Euery one gone.

Who will buy a poeme *cia do cheinneóchadh dán*? Now that
The wynde has died doune and the calendar daies outnumbered
To enclowd the dark secrets of the errant-runners, the braggarts?
Who will buy a poeme Now that the great oak woods haue been felled,

The game and cuckoo song banished from ancient Aherlow; Now
That the poets are forced to beggar them selues as rymers pencilling
Soured sonnets to the livery of Popingyes wont to playe the king,
Bending the knee to new Customes of mimicry and rime; Now

For the moste part at a loss to offer Sanctuarie to the wylde wordes
Al of a scatter lyke dandelion floss counted out in hovrs of the clock
And outlawed lyke a swarme of Gnats from the Bog of Allen:
The canker of contrarie Speache granted thus to halter and sword, to

The machinations of those with a trick or two vp the sleeve,
The knave, the black heart, the ace of spades. On my worde.

Ceist! Cia do cheinneóchadh dán? / Who will buy a poem?
The poet Mathghamhain Ó hIfearnáin, early C17th

276

Liam Guilar   *Akhmatova's Requiem*
(After the Lesson)

Such grief might make the mountains weep,
It pounded on the anvil of your patience,
sparking poems as you shuffled through the snow.

A memory of terror echoes
like the midnight knock on someone else's door.
But the Wall is down, the Empire folded, your enemies
mere footnotes to your history, while the words
you dared not write on paper lie
discarded on my classroom floor.

Jeanette McCullough

Joseph Cummins   *This Is Not a Poem*

This is not a poem
About politics, Americans or religion.
I won't talk about beauty or ugliness.
I'm not interested in the vibe or the nation's stirring issues.
I'm not going to be right wing or left wing, I prefer to hide in centre stage.
I shan't be describing glowing sunsets over sparkling beaches.
Or debating global terrorism.
Or violence
Or hate
Or death.
And I certainly won't be mentioning happiness, heartache, pain or joy.
I won't talk about love,
Or how it feels to be alone,
I will not express emotion,
Because this is not a poem.

This does not have any time or rhythm patterns,
Or a constant rhyming scheme,
Little bursts of rhyme in places, but the rest just doesn't fit,
It's awkward, not smooth or easy, flowing only because it has to.
Doesn't necessarily have a particular message to convey,
It's not a clear cut story,
Got no theme, no mood, no tone,
Don't expect a point, remember,
This is not a poem.

So remember when it happens,
Remember reading this today,
There are things they'll stop you doing,
Games they won't let you play.
There are things that you can't mention,
Truths that they won't let you say,
Things won't go in steady rhythm,
Things won't rhyme and go your way.

There won't be messages or morals,
And you'll feel you're on your own,
But everyone knows this feeling,
Because life is not a poem.

Conor Kelly   *Padraic Colum's Lectures on Modern Irish Poetry*

My eyelids are heavy and red
From straining at my VDU,
I've put my lectures on the screen –
Planter and Gael in Montague.
I'll read that one in Aberdeen.
       The one on Heaney's bound for Rome.
       Displacement and the Rural Home.

And I must fly the routes between
The lecture and the seminar
To talk on *Marx and Late MacNeice*
In Austria or Zanzibar
Or at a conference in Greece.
       Another speech I must rehearse
       Is *Politics and Irish Verse.*

Professor Zlot in Prague inquires,
'Was Clarke a deconstructionist?
Was Devlin of the Eliot school?
Is Beckett's verse post-modernist?
Does Durcan not unduly drool?
       A crowded lecture hall awaits
       Your views on poets after Yeats.'

And what, to me, is this lit-crit?
Sometimes, in flight, I watch a cloud
Float underneath the starboard wing
And think of feelings disallowed,
Of songs my mother used to sing.
       I think, sometimes, I would prefer
       To sell cattle at a Longford fair.

Mo Ryan   *Dear William . . .*

. . . This is just to say
not much depends
upon red wheelbarrows
anymore.

The rain is acid now,
its glaze gnaws paint,
and metal holes
shed flakes of rust.

Next door's retired greyhound
ate two of the white chickens.
One died egg bound.
They culled the rest – bird flu.

And you know
those plums,
so delicious,
cold and sweet
I was saving
for my breakfast?

I gashed my leg
on a rust flecked edge,
hoisting the barrow
into the green skip
from Western Waste.
Reacted with boils and fever
to the Tetanus shot.

The red plums
decomposed,
bloated, split, leaked
sweet brown fluids
on to the
white icebox.

Forgive me.

'William' is the American poet William Carlos Williams (1883–1963)

MUSIC

Liam Aungier   *Postlude*

'… *a Gould recording of a Bach prelude and fugue was launched into*
space on Voyager in 1977 to instruct aliens about human culture …'
— New York Review of Books, October 7th, 2004

It isn't true. Our history was never well-tempered
Despite what all these notes may tell.
Conflict, not counterpoint, was our passion,
Alongside *Erbarme dich*, Bergen-Belsen.

But being human how could we resist
A temptation to boast, to fling our greatest art
To the interstellar void and let it drift
Past solar winds, dark matters? And yet

This fugue has flown light-years for your hearing,
Incline to its sound your vague inhuman ear,
You'll learn its grace, its subtle harmonies.
It's the best of us, it's what we might have been.

Edwin Smith

John Prior *Gordon*

The rain on the leaves
outside Gordon's room
seemed to be leaking in.
The windows steamy and the air
smelling of stale St Bruno
and brilliantine.

Mahler was on his player.
I thought it was Mahler
or perhaps it was Verdi's Requiem –
I didn't know much about music then.
His pipe sat in a saucer on the arm
of the threadbare chair he sat in.

He got up to turn the record over,
his creased brown trousers bunched on desert boots.
Mahler had such a peculiar love life, he said.
In the kitchen someone
was finishing last night's dishes –
an aluminium saucepan and some glasses.

Do you know about Mahler? he asked me,
starting the hi-fi again.
Outside a sparrow
on the leaky leaves
cold and wet. I'm thinking,
what does he know of love?

Ted Deppe   *House of Hospitality*

Tivoli, New York, 1976

Down the hall, someone's playing Schumann and cursing,
and Dorothy says, 'That's why we call this a house
of hostility. At least we don't turn away those in need,
but all our farms are failures.' She quotes Dostoyevsky
to sum up fifty years of the Worker: 'Love in dreams
seems easy, but love in action is a harsh and dreadful thing.'

Outside, the ice on the Hudson keeps breaking with loud booms,
and Dorothy recalls the San Francisco quake
when she was eight. Which prompts an elderly man, silent so far,
to clear his throat and say, 'I was there – I heard Caruso
sing from the window of the Palace Hotel. We were running
down Market Street when Mother stopped, pointed up,

and there he was, testing his voice, they say – he was afraid
he might have lost it during the disaster – singing from *La Bohème*,
that magnificent tenor of his floating above the sound of collapsing
buildings.' 'And you heard him sing?' asks Dorothy, 'you heard
Caruso?' and the man – a very articulate schizophrenic – says,
 'I saw a city destroyed and heard Caruso sing on the same morning.'

'What a life!' Dorothy says. 'See, I was in Oakland,
where it wasn't so bad. I only read about Caruso. And his valet –
did you see him? A character out of Ignazio Silone!
I mean, I love opera, I love Caruso, but this valet, when the quake hit,
reportedly came into the maestro's hotel room
and told him, 'Signor, it is nothing – nothing – but I think

we should go outside.' Then, once he'd waited in the shaking
building for Caruso to sing, *a capella*, the complete aria,
once he'd finally escorted him safely to the open square,
he climbed six floors to that Room with a View
to pack the great man's trunks, and carefully – apparently
calmly – carried them down, one by one.'

Niall McGrath   *Paralytic*

'The ingenious Mr Handell is very much indispos'd
and it's thought with a Paralytick Disorder...'
– London Evening Standard, *May 1737*

The media can be cruel
but perhaps the cartoonists were right
to depict him as a pig;
though his reason for leaving
friends at a dinner party
supping on paltry fare
(showbiz a poor investment)
while he binged in the pantry
on delicacies he'd denied them
and a hamper of burgundy
might be explained by
exposure to lead:
in wig powder, food,
or as a preservative in port.
It pained and turned his head,
made him into a brute,
irritable with singers,
blind in one eye,
upsetting his stomach
all the while he craved
that which was poisoning him.

Then came the stroke
that stilled corpulent fingers;
altered his outlook –
no longer operas characterised
by gods and heroes,
down to earth now,
mere mortals facing tragedies,
curtailed in oratorios.
Doctors and friends had urged him
to tackle his obesity;

having failed to overcome
his own demons, he created
the mysterious grandeur
of *Susanna, Joshua*
and *Israel in Egypt,*
the ironic otherness of the *Messiah.*

ART

Moyra Donaldson   *Hogarth – Self-Portrait with Pug*
Irish Museum of Modern Art 2007

Who is this and what is she doing here
like a distorting mirror, looking at me
as if I am not me but her; a different time,
but still with my pug beside me and still
gin lane, the fallen women, the marriage *à la*

mode. I've been kind to myself, but she knows
how it is: outside it is raining and as the needle
disappears into the grey sky, the same things
are happening that have always happened,
and nothing is so black and white that it is

not lived in vividness. I'm only part of this,
and so is she and those she's with, the figures
beside her, behind her, inside her, jostling,
casting a shadow backwards to what lies
before us all, and the whole line up of us

knows it's about flesh, its influence, the demands
it makes upon us, its hungers and requirements;
how it makes us who we are, despite our desire
to be something lighter: it holds us to ourselves.
Ballast to our souls, our blood looks through.

Jenny Vuglar   *Jerome 3: Otium*

The poem takes as its starting point the painting
Jerome in his Study *by Antonello da Messina*
in the National Gallery, London.

His outdoor patens are at the bottom of the stairs
under that red robe he is barefoot
feeling the smooth wood with the soles of his feet
flexing and unflexing his toes.

Summer has come in. On the lake two men row,
the water sliding under their oars,
the boat drifting. The birds beat their wings
in ecstasy, singing up into the open sky.

When Jerome turns the page everything is in abeyance.
The oars are still, the birds held on his breath;

his sighing breath that lets the world run on,
the velum under his fingers
the words decorously spilt. He rolls
each thought around his tongue. Sweet words.
Sweet reason. The sun catches the page.

Colin Pink   *Five Painters*

Giotto
A perfect O free hand
feet flat on the land
beneath a solid blue sky.

Piero
Eyes that stare through
resurrect sacred geometry's
plumb line to the unseen.

Leonardo
Within a deluge of lines
forms of life coalesce
but will never be finished.

Rembrandt
The weight of a life
held within the viscous
glisten of a brush stroke.

Pollock
The way life brimmed up
it was bound to get spilt
but left skeins of beauty.

Sue Rose   *Caravaggio's Virgin*

I hadn't met anyone like him before –
all I had to do was play dead; much easier
than pacing the narrow dark
round Piazza Navona, heels stabbing
at the stairs of bridges, arches strained.

My red shoes glowed like lanterns
in the corner of the room, my bare feet froze;
I couldn't breathe for the reek of pigments,
the scarlet drapes blooming
in the candlelight, taking all the air.

He told me red was the only true colour
the colour of sex, joked about the death
of the Virgin in a shift of reds, the symbolism
of bare feet, mocking the pilgrims on their way
to sanctuary. There is no deliverance,
he said, no Assumption.

He wouldn't show me at first,
the canvas turned against the wall.
He coloured my skin instead, a flush
of heat livening the grain of my body
beneath the canopy, his strokes sure.

He said he loved me
but he was a liar – look at me
lying there, bloated, hair dull,
hemmed in by a bevy of old men,
any fallen woman fished from the Tiber,
soles blackened by walking the streets.

Geraldine Mills   *Mrs Monet Cleans the Lily Pond*

She trawls her net across the green rash of weed,
he watching her from the window in a frenzy
so that he will not lift a brush, a palate knife
until she's done, her dress flounced into her pantaloons
a hat protecting her from the Givergny sun.

In the gather of slime, she sees picnics plein air
with Mrs Renoir, Pissarro though they don't see
eye to eye on dress fabrics or ducks' livers,
Mrs Cezanne a bit too dry for her taste
and yet she has a soft reasoning at the dinner table
when tempers rise, a glass knocked over
spills its red stain upon the white damask
and a voice gravels from beyond.

Her net fills with the smell of rotting.
She dredges newts out of their philanderings,
a silt of caddis world, of wandering snail,
a leech puckers to the cold skin of her calf
until the water ripples out its surface tension
and all he sees are blooms full and pert as divas.

Susan Millar DuMars   *Madame Matisse is Shown*
Her Portrait, 1913

Whose is this face?
A pebble thrown in a pond,
sinking grey over black over grey,
further and further away.

Whose are these hands?
Fingers unfinished; flippers to flap
around garden and house.
My hands are stronger than that.
Counted coins, wrote ferocious letters,
once. Don't you remember?

Why that hat?
With blushing rose
and peacock feather.
What does that sexless creature
need with a Paris hat?
Why not a dowager's veil,
a housemaid's cap?
Why not a wimple and beads,
my Lord!
The better to toil toward
your veneration.

I'm a good disciple, you will allow –
everybody loves you now.

Why these tears? Why this feeling I'm sinking?
Portrait of Madame Matisse. Who is she?
Henri, my love, my dear old friend.
When did you stop seeing me?

Liz McSkeane   *Life Class*

The teacher says, forget the outlines, try
for depth in shadings to catch the tension
of suppressed movement and dimensions
you don't see. Politics of the body.
I just don't get it. I half-close my eyes
and the whole thing shifts to a new version,
another meaning. Tricks of perception
like this bother me, make me doubt what I
see: I can't tell how things should be looked at,
interpreted, pinned down. The outlines
give me trouble, starting with the skin,
then the space we have to negotiate
between my viewpoint and yours, what defines
where my boundaries end, and yours begin.

Paul Stubbs   *En Route to Bethlehem*

after 'Study of Human Body from a Drawing by Ingres' 1982

The beast he makes a detour, plunges
into the Irish sea, heads for the base

of Ben Bulben, where one religion later,
we catch up with him, slumped

against the gravestone of Yeats –
horrified to be left alone...

Tom French   *A Limousine at Carrigillihy*

For twenty summers in his hearse parked
on Mary O'Driscoll's grass that gives
onto treacherous rocks named
'The Treacherous Rocks', a pair of islands
going by 'Adam' and 'Eve' where the cattle
are herded by the sea, that you can see
from Mary's south-facing settee,
Charlie Shearer slept the sleep of the dead.

He sleeps upstairs like one of the family now
while his paintings of the house he sleeps in
hang downstairs. In a corner of the garden
in one, under flowering Buddleia, is the car,
the driver's window lowered to let in air,
where Charlie has painted himself asleep,
dreaming of painting where a corpse would be.

David Grubb   *When You Take a Photograph*

When you take a photograph you lift light
and lay it on a surface.
When you lift light you trick time and
grandmother in the garden remains there
for perhaps sixty or seventy years and her smile
and the sound of the five geese.
When you catch time like this perhaps even God
is unsure as to whether this is real or dreaming real
or is this what the human can do with matter? If this is so
then the actuality of miracles is surpassed. When you have
made a miracle you cannot take a photograph of it because
it is beyond light and it will never stay still until you yourself
have gone beyond these sounds and trees and racing days.

Michael Massey   *Ann*

Everything in place: his arm
warm on her shoulders, his heart
pulsing in her ear, her yellow dress
whispering to the long grass, the sun
poised above willow trees that drip
green into the river. Cows raise heavy
heads, stare with liquid eyes. Swallows
scythe through June heat, skim the river.

He harvests these elements, stores
them till a flickering candle casts
his hunched shadow to the wall
and his fertile quill feeds them
back to virgin paper: *Shall I
compare thee to a summer's day...*

David Wheatley   *Miranda*

Who is hiding from whom, you or the world
beyond your sea coast issueless as Bohemia's?
Not that the spell has failed, but has worked too well:
discarded chesspieces knee-deep in sand
along a beach lacking only the flagpoles and pier
to pass for an out-of-season Courtown or Bray,
your tights and blouses hung out to dry between
two trees while gibberish Caliban scowls at his pool,
the magical commonplace long since become
commonplace magic. Miranda, I've had enough too:
let me surprise you by failing the next time I try
to conjure a playing card from behind your ear
or an egg from your palm. Behind a shifting sand dune
that you pass every day and have never explored
my life-boat is waiting patiently for you,
and waiting in the long grass a suitcase packed
for your departure to somewhere disenchantingly
new in ways you could only marvel at now.

Will Johnson   *The Seagull from 16 to 60*

i.m. TP McKenna

The last year before my proper life began
you were already plotting in your book,
as actors should, not your own thoughts
but those of Trigorin with an Irish brogue –
enough to alert me to that sardonic strain
of self-effacement when it came to art.
But for all your charm I wanted Nina
to love the widowed mother's son
since that was me – or so I thought.

A brief entr'acte – Konstantin
shot himself in nineteen-sixty-eight.
Trigorin scribbled on for forty years;
some nights I'd see him
mouthing in that corner by the lamp,
Nina too, although we never spoke.

Today, if anyone, I'm you as you were then
that final matinee in an echoing rep,
which makes me nearly no-one at a stroke,
a visitor from an off-stage world
that can't exist. But if you'll forgive
the indiscretion, take this note:
work from the uncut text alone, try not
to corpse until your lines run dry, exit
with a flourish to the vacant gods,
and only then bring up the lamps and board
the train for Dublin, Moscow, and
beyond this gauze, the endless, moonlit steppe.

Ian Wild   *Harpo*

Who needs words cherubic tramp?
Enough are the music and laughter
of silver spoons cascading from your sleeves,
the larks in your fingers, blurring arpeggios
on strings of Grou cho's

wo   rds.

Grouc ho's wor wo wor

Hey, will you cut it out with those scissors?

When I was too small to kick the world in the pants
you did it for me. Now you are gone,
I boot for both of us, listening for silent
laughter in Heaven.

Womanstruck Gabriel
does God even know he is holding your leg?
that *his* halo is burning in the popcorn stand?

that that

stop eating my wor

eating my

eati

part of a horn

silence.

Notes on Contributors

NB: Considerable effort has been made to contact each individual contributor who appears in this anthology. Inevitably, we were often unable to do so and therefore had to rely on information in the public domain in some cases. Apologies in advance for any errors that have been inadvertently included which we will happily correct in subsequent printings.

Poets and Translators

James Aitchison (SHOp #43, 2013) was born in Stirlingshire in 1938. He has published several collections of poems and the critical study, *The Golden Harvester: The Vision of Edwin Muir.*

Gabrielle Alioth (SHOp #6, 2001) is a Swiss novelist living in County Louth. Her poem here was the first she ever had published.

Gary Allen (SHOp #33, 2010) is a poet and novelist from Ballymena, County Antrim.

Joseph Allen (SHOp #25, 2007) is a poet and Delta Blues musician from Ballymena, County Antrim.

David Andrew (SHOp #42, 2013) has published two collections of poetry and volunteers with the poetry website www.writeoutloud.net.

Arlene Ang (SHOp #27, 2008) was born in Manilaand currently lives in Spinea, Italy. She is the author of *The Desecration of Doves* (2005) and has been nominated five times for the Pushcart Prize.

Dermot J. Archer (SHOp #25, 2007) is a former lecturer in Literature and Creative Writing and Associate Lecturer at Queen's University.

Liam Aungier (SHOp #29, 2009) lives in County Kildare and works in Dublin as a civil servant.

David Ball (SHOp #35, 2011) is Professor Emeritus of French Language & Literature and Comparative Literature at Smith College in Massachusetts, currently living in France.

Ivy Bannister (SHOp #12) was educated at Smith College and Trinity College in Dublin. Her poetry and short stories have appeared in various anthologies of Irish writing.

Leland Bardwell (SHOp #11, 2003) was an Irish poet, novelist, and playwright. She was born in India to Irish parents and moved to Ireland at the age of two. She died in 2016.

Sebastian Barker (SHOp #29, 2009) was a British poet who has been compared to William Blake. He was Chairman of the Poetry Society from 1988-92 and died in 2014.

Alex Barr (SHOp #12, 2003) is a poet, playwright and short story writer who runs a smallholding in Pembrokeshire.

Michael Bartholomew-Biggs (SHOp #13, 2003) is a semi-retired mathematician and fully-active poet who lives in London. He is poetry editor of the on-line magazine *London Grip*.

Neil Bedford (SHOp #7, 2001) is a retired college lecturer enjoying the quiet life in West Clare

Oliver Bernard (SHOp #7, 2001) was a poet and translator, best known for his translations of Rimbaud in the Penguin Classics collection. He died in 2013, aged 87.

Paul Birtill (SHOp #26, 2008) was born in Liverpool and is half-Irish. His most recent books is *New and Selected Poems*, published in 2015.

Denise Blake (SHOp #26, 2008) is a poet, writer and creative writing facilitator. She also records prose pieces for *Sunday Miscellany* on RTÉ Radio.

Gerry Boland (SHOp #24, 2007) is a poet and author who lives in north Roscommon. He regularly leads workshops for adults and children.

Pat Boran (SHOp #35, 2011) is the publisher of the Dedalus Press which specialises in contemporary poetry from Ireland, and international poetry in English-language translation.

Eva Bourke (SHOp #28, 2008) is a German-born Irish poet and translator with seven collections published. She is a member of Aosdána.

Alison Brackenbury (SHOp #40, 2012) is an officially retired British poet inexplicably busy with plants, animals and poetry readings.

Peter Branson (SHOp #44, 2014) is a full-time poet, songwriter, singer and socialist from East Cheshire.

Colm Breathnach (SHOp #30, 2009) is a Cork-born poet, novelist and translator who writes in both Irish and English.

Deirdre Brennan (SHOp #9, 2002) is a bilingual poet, playwright and writer of short stories.

Nick Bridson Baker is an ex-cartoonist, now doing monotype prints and paintings in his shed. His poems have been published in a number of magazines.

Christine Broe (SHOp #8, 2002) is Dublin-born and worked as an art teacher and art therapist before writing poetry in the 1990s. She won the inaugural Brendan Kennelly Award in 2001.

Pamela Mary Brown (SHOp #42, 2013) is from Donegal and currently is Writer in Residence at HMP Magilligan and Editor of *Time In* prison magazine.

Alan Brownjohn FRSL (SHOp #15, 2004) is an English poet and novelist who has also worked as a teacher, lecturer, critic and broadcaster.

Sam Burnside (SHOp #46, 2014) was born in County Antrim and now lives and works in the city of Derry where he was founder and first Director of the Verbal Arts Centre.

Paddy Bushe (SHOp #2, 2000) was born in Dublin and now lives in Kerry. He is a poet, editor and translator. *On a Turning Wing* (2016) won the Irish Times Poetry Now Award.

Maggie Butt (SHOp #20, 2006) is an ex-journalist and BBC TV producer turned poet and novelist.

Michael Casey (SHOp #46, 2014) was born in Naas and now lives in Dublin. An economist by training, he found it relatively easy to makes the transition to literature, his first love.

John Wedgwood Clarke (SHOp #42, 2013) is a poet, writer, editor and Senior Lecturer in Creative Writing at the University of Exeter.

Harry Clifton (SHOp #46, 2014) has published ten books of poetry and lectured at University College Dublin until last year. He was the Fifth Ireland Professor of Poetry from 2010-2013.

Marguerite Colgar (SHOp #25, 2007) no information available.

Albert Conneely (SHOp #28, 2008) has had poems published in *Dream Catcher*, *Stinging Fly* and in a few one-edition wonders. He studied English at York, England, and lives in Dun Laoghaire.

Noel Conneely (SHOp #46, 2014) has had poems published in *Chelsea*, *Willow Review*, *The Coe Review* and other publications in Ireland and the UK. He works as a teacher in Dublin.

Susan Connolly (SHOp #26, 2008) is from Drogheda, County Louth and won the Patrick and Katherine Kavanagh Fellowship in Poetry in 2001.

Jim Conwell (SHOp #41, 2013) is a poet who lives and works in London. With an original background in Fine Art, he has worked in the field of mental health for the past 25 years.

Stephanie Conybeare (SHOp #45, 2014) has published fiction and three collections of poetry, the most recent entitled *Risk*. Canadian-born she currently divides her time between London and France.

Frances Cotter (SHOp #22, 2006) teaches English in Kilkenny. Her poems have been published in various magazines and she received the Annie Deaney Memorial Prize.

Patrick Cotter (SHOp #46, 2014) is a poet based in Cork City and the Artistic Director of the Munster Literature Centre.

A.M. Cousins (SHOp #46, 2014) has lived in Wexford town since 1982. She won the FISH International Poetry prize in 2019 for a poem called 'Not My Michael Furey'.

Derek Coyle (SHOp #33, 2010) is a lecturer in English at Carlow College whose poems have been shortlisted for the Patrick Kavanagh Award (2010, 2014) and the Bradshaw Prize (2011, 2013).

Enda Coyle-Greene (SHOp #14, 2004) is co-founder and Artistic Director of the Fingal Poetry Festival. Her third collection of poetry came from Dedalus in February 2020.

Kevin Crossley-Holland (SHOp #39, 201 2) is an English translator, children's author and poet.

Seth Crook (SHOp #43, 2013) taught philosophy at various universities in the US for a number of years, and then moved to the Isle of Mull and became devoted to poetry.

Joseph Cummins (SHOp #19, 2005) was sixteen when his poem, his only notable publication, appeared in the magazine. Now 31, he lives in Dublin.

Michael Curtis (SHOp #19, 2005) lives in Kent and the Isle of Man. He has given readings, workshops and residencies in England, Ireland, France, Belgium, Finland, Latvia and Germany.

Julia Dale (SHOp #13, 2003) is a translator and poet. Born in the UK, she studied literature at Oxford and Cambridge Universities.

Daniel Daly (SHOp #28, 2008) since retirement is enjoying freedom, music, wine and writing more poetry.

N. Daly (SHOp #27, 2008) no information available.

John Daniel (SHOp #29, 2009) has published four books of poetry and two volumes of autobiography, *Grown-up War* and *No Man's Land*. He lives in Eynsham near Oxford.

Miriam Darlington (SHOp #25, 2007) lectures in Creative Writing at Plymouth University and writes the 'Nature Notebook' column in *The Times*. Her latest book is *Owl Sense*.

Michael Davitt (SHOp #19, 2005) was a poet who published in Irish. He has been characterised as a key figure in the 1970s Irish language poetry movement. He died in 2005.

Gerald Dawe (SHOp #44, 2014) was Professor in English at TCD and the inaugural director of the Oscar Wilde Centre for Irish Writing. He has published 20 books of poetry and prose.

Ann Dean (SHOp #19, 2005) no information available.

John F. Deane (SHOp #39, 2012) is an Irish poet and novelist who was the founder of *Poetry Ireland* and *The Poetry Ireland Review*. He has published thirteen collections of poetry.

Celia de Fréine (SHOp #12, 2003) was born in County Down and is a poet, playwright, screenwriter and librettist who writes in Irish and English. Her poem here is one of her favourites.

Greg Delanty (SHOp #5, 2001), translator of Liam Ó Muirthile, is a celebrated poet on both sides of the Atlantic. His latest book is *No More Time,* LSU Press, Oct 2020 (www.eurospangroup.com).

Edward Denniston (SHOp #6, 2001) was born in Longford and attended Trinity College Dublin. He has lived in Waterford since 1980, where he teaches in the Newtown School.

Ted Deppe (SHOp #6, 2001) is the author of seven books of poems and teaches in the Stonecoast MFA programme in Portland, Maine.

Stephen Devereux (SHOp #37, 2011) has published poetry, short stories, critical essays and travel writing. He was runner-up in the Elmet Foundation Ted Hughes Poetry Prize.

Moyra Donaldson (SHOp #28, 2008) was born County Down and attended Queen's University Belfast and the University of Ulster. She is a retired social worker.

Theo Dorgan (SHOp #2, 2000) is a poet, nonfiction prose writer, novelist, editor, documentary screenwriter, essayist, librettist and translator. He won the 1992 Listowel Prize for Poetry and the 2015 Poetry Now Award.

Tom Duddy (SHOp #16, 2004) was a poet, philosopher, and a senior lecturer at NUI Galway. He died in 2012.

Siobhan Duffy (SHOp #36, 2011) is an Irish poet and critic. Author of six collections, she has developed writing workshops for military veterans and story-gathering protocols for work with refugees.

Frank Dullaghan (SHOp #8, 2002) is an Irish poet who lives in Dubai, UAE, where he is Head of Compliance for a small mining company.

Marie Dullagh (SHOp #46, 2014) is a reluctant wanderer, anchored to sanity by a pen and a camera.

Susan Millar DuMars (SHOp #41, 2013) was born and raised in Philadelphia to a Belfast mother. In 1997 she visited Galway during the Galway Arts Festival and has since made the city her home.

Mary Durkin (SHOp #17, 2005) lives and writes in Northumberland.

Martin Dyar (SHOp #39, 2012) grew up in County Mayo. His won the Patrick Kavanagh Poetry Award in 2009 and the Strokestown International Poetry Award in 2001.

Hilary Elfick (SHOp #19, 2005) has published a novel and over 20 collections of poetry, three of which have been published bilingually in Romania.

Julian Farmer (SHOp #32, 2010) is a poet and translator from several languages, especially French, Classical Greek, Latin, Russian and now a little Chinese. He lives in Guildford in the UK.

Alana Farrell (SHOp #36, 2011) no information available.

Frank Farrelly (SHOp #41, 2013) is from Waterford and his poems have appeared in *Poetry Ireland Review, The Moth, Crannog, Stinging Fly, The Honest Ulsterman* and other magazines.

Mary Ellen Fean (SHOp #37, 2011) lives in Galway City and has had her poetry published in *Cyphers* (Dublin), *The Clare Champion* and *The Galway Review*, among others.

Geraldine Finn (SHOp #16, 2004) no information available.

Gabriel Fitzmaurice (SHOp #12, 2003) lives in the village of Moyvane, County Kerry. He is author of more than fifty books, including collections of poetry in English and Irish.

Leontia Flynn (SHOp #46, 2014) has worked at The Seamus Heaney Centre for Poetry at Queen's University Belfast since 2005. She received the Rooney Prize for Irish Literature in 2008.

Roderick Ford (SHOp #26, 2008) is a poet and playwright whose work explores themes of otherness and othering, of voicelessness and estrangement.

Angela France (SHOp #27, 2008) has been studying, reading, writing, and teaching poetry for the past twenty years. She lives in Cheltenham in the UK.

Tom French (SHOp #46, 2014) lives with his family in County Meath, where he earns his living in the county library service. In 2016 he won the Lawrence O'Shaughnessy Award for Poetry.

Anne-Marie Fyfe (SHOp #45, 2014) is a poet, creative writing teacher and arts organiser. She lives in West London where she runs the Coffee-House Poetry reading and workshop series.

Owen Gallagher (SHOp #43, 2013) is originally from The Gorbals, Glasgow and now lives in London. His poetry has received awards from the London Arts Board and The Society of Authors.

Peggie Gallagher (SHOp #34, 2010) lives in Sligo and her collection *Tilth* was published in 2013. Her work has been published in *Poetry Ireland, Force 10, Atlanta Review* and *Envoi*, among others.

Patrick Galvin (SHOp #36, 2011) was an Irish poet, singer, playwright and screenwriter. Born in Cork's inner city in 1927, he died in 2011.

Sam Gardiner (SHOp #35, 2011), who died in 2016, was a distinguished member of the generation of Northern Irish poets that also included Seamus Heaney, Michael Longley and Derek Mahon.

Denise Garvey (SHOp #32, 2010) directs a maths and English study centre in Galway. Her work has been published by *Happiness is Vital, Skylight 47* and elsewhere.

Rebecca Gethin (SHOp #36, 2011) lives on Dartmoor in Devon and writes passionately about species extinction. *Vanishings*, published in 2020, is her fourth poetry collection.

Peter Gill (SHOp #37, 2011) is a poet and playwright. Born in 1939 in Cardiff he started his career as an actor and has also directed over 100 productions in the UK, Europe and North America.

Ray Givans (SHOp #16, 2004) taught English in secondary schools in County Down. He is a member of the Queen's Writers' Group at the Seamus Heaney Centre in Belfast.

Frank Golden (SHOp #42, 2013) was born in Dublin and has been living in the Burren for over twenty years. His poetry collection *In Daily Accord* was published in 2008.

Lizann Gorman (SHOp #26, 2008) lives in the West of Ireland and has a Master's in Poetry Studies. She has been published in a number of journals both in print and online.

Colin Graham (SHOp #35, 2011) is Professor and Head of English at Maynooth University. He is the author of *Deconstructing Ireland* (2001) and co-editor of *The Irish Review*.

Kevin Graham (SHOp #44, 2014) lives and works in Dublin. His recent poems have appeared in *The Stinging Fly*, *Causeway/Cabhsair* and *Crannóg*.

Ann Gray (SHOp #23, 2007) has a Creative Writing MA from the University of Plymouth. Her collection *At the Gate* was published in 2008. She won the Ballymaloe Poetry Prize in 2014.

John Greening (SHOp #33, 2010) is a poet, critic and editor. Ted Hughes and Seamus Heaney selected 'The Coastal Path' to be in the top six for the Observer Arvon poetry competition in 1987.

Eamon Grennan (SHOp #11, 2003) is an Irish poet born in Dublin. He was the Dexter M. Ferry Jr. Professor of English at Vassar College until his retirement in 2004.

Vona Groarke (SHOp #19, 2005) was born in Mostrim in the Irish midlands and attended Trinity College Dublin and University College Cork. She has published five collections of poetry.

David Grubb (SHOp #23, 2007) received third prize in the 2006 National Poetry Competition for his poem 'Bud Fields and His World'. His poetry collections include *Ways of Looking* (2013).

Liam Guilar (SHOp #46, 2014) studied Medieval History and Literature at Birmingham University and and has a PhD from Deakin University. He has published six collections of poetry.

Atar Hadari (SHOp #8, 2002) was born in Israel and raised in England. He won a scholarship to study poetry and playwriting with Derek Walcott at Boston University.

Richard W. Halperin (SHOp #27, 2008) holds Irish and US nationality and lives in Paris. Recent poetry collections are *Catch Me While You Have the Light* (2018) and *Luna Moth & Jacob's Ladder* (2019).

Robert Hamberger (SHOp #44, 2014) has had poems appear in British, American and Japanese anthologies. His fourth collection, *Blue Wallpaper,* has been shortlisted for the 2020 Polari Prize.

Sheila Hamilton (SHOp #46, 2014) has lived in Hungary and Scotland. She has had poems published in *The Rialto* and *Poetry London* among others, and currently lives in northwest England.

James Harpur (SHOp #18, 2005) has had six poetry collections published, including *The White Silhouette* (2018), an Irish Times Book of the Year. He lives in Clonakilty in County Cork.

Maggie Harris (SHOp #16, 2004) is a poet, prose writer and visual artist. She has twice won the Guyana Prize for poetry and was Caribbean Winner of the Commonwealth Short Story Prize.

Ian Harrow (SHOp #46, 2014) was born in 1945 in Northumberland, of Scots-Irish extraction. Since the mid-1970s his work has appeared in a wide range of publications. He lives in York.

Michael Hartnett (SHOp #10, 2002) was an Irish poet who wrote in both English and Irish. He has been called 'Munster's de facto poet laureate'. He died in 1999.

Anne Haverty (SHOp #14, 2004) is an Irish novelist and poet. Educated at Trinity College Dublin and the Sorbonne, her novel *One Day as a Tiger* won the Rooney Prize for Irish Literature in 1997.

Aidan Hayes (SHOp #34, 2010) has worked variously as an actor and as a teacher at schools, colleges and prisons. In 1995 he won the Listowel Writers' Week Prize for Best Single Poem.

Seamus Heaney (SHOp #5, 2001) was a poet, playwright and translator. In 1995 he received the Nobel Prize in Literature. He has been described as 'the most important poet since Yeats'. He died in 2013.

Todd Hearon (SHOp #10, 2002), translator of Michael Hartnett, is a poet and songwriter living in Exeter, New Hampshire.

Áine Herlihy (SHOp #26, 2008) no information available.

Seán Hewitt (SHOp #40, 2012) is a book critic for *The Irish Times* and teaches Modern British & Irish Literature at Trinity College. His book *J.M. Synge: Nature, Politics, Modernism* is forthcoming.

Kevin Higgins (SHOp #40, 2012) lives in Galway. He won the 2003 Cúirt Festival Poetry Grand Slam and was awarded a literature bursary by the Arts Council of Ireland in 2005.

Rita Ann Higgins (SHOp #31, 2009) is a poet, playwright and editor from Galway. She has published 10 collections of poetry and a memoir.

Seamus Hogan (SHOp #42, 2013) was a poet and pig farmer from Ballydehob, County Cork who once lived in the iconic bookshop, Shakespeare & Co, in Paris. He died in 2017.

Margaret Holbrook (SHOp #45, 2014) is an author, poet, and playwright who lives in Cheshire in the UK.

Joseph Horgan (SHOp #18, 2005) was in Birmingham and has lived in Cork since 1999. He has won the Patrick Kavanagh Award and was short-listed for a Hennessy Award.

Kaarina Hollo (SHOp #45, 2014) is a lecturer in Irish in the School of English. Her research focuses on literary cultures of Ireland and literary translation in the Irish context.

Angela Howarth Marks (SHOp #20, 2006) no information available.

Cate Huguelet (SHOp #31, 2009) began as a travel and food writer before leaving Chicago for an internship at *The Dubliner* magazine. She has a PhD in English from University College Cork.

Bruce James (SHOp #36, 2011) was a poet, artist, musician and potter of Welsh, Irish and French descent. He died soon after this poem was published in 2011.

Christine James (SHOp #25, 2007) is a Welsh poet and academic who was Archdruid of Wales from June 2013 until June 2016, the first woman to hold the title.

Maureen Jivani (SHOp #33, 2010) has published poems in the United Kingdom, the United States of America, New Zealand and Australia in both online and print magazines.

Will Johnson (SHOp #40, 2012) lives with his family in Cardiff. His poems have appeared in numerous magazines and anthologies, including *Poetry Salzburg Review* and *Poetry Wales*.

Fred Johnston (SHOp #15, 2004) is an Irish poet, novelist, literary critic and musician. He founded Galway's Cúirt International Festival of Literature in 1986.

Jenny Joseph (SHOp #1, 1999) was an English poet, best known for the poem that begins 'When I am an old woman I shall wear purple …' which in her old age she disliked. She died in 2018.

Pat Jourdan (SHOp #21, 2006) graduated from Liverpool College of Art. She is now a painter living in Galway where she is the Editor of *The Lantern Review*.

Ilya Kaminsky (SHOp #32, 2010) is a Ukrainian-Russian-Jewish-American poet, critic, translator and professor. His poetry collections include *Dancing in Odessa* and *Deaf Republic*.

Anthony Keating (SHOp #7, 2001) is Senior Lecturer, Psychosocial Analysis of Offending Behaviour, Faculty of Health and Social care, Edge Hill University, Lancashire, UK.

Conor Kelly (SHOp #44, 2014) is an Irish writer living in a rural area of West Clare. He has had poems printed in *Poetry Ireland Review, The Irish Times, The Sunday Tribune* and elsewhere.

Richard Kemp (SHOp #16, 2004) no information available.

Kevin Kiely (SHOp #21, 2006) is a poet, critic and novelist born in County Down. He received a PhD in Modernist Poetry from University College Dublin.

Sheila Killian (SHOp #20, 2006) is a professor at the Kemmy Business School, University of Limerick. She teaches corporate finance and corporate social responsibility.

Noel King (SHOp #31, 2009) was born and lives in Tralee, County Kerry. His poems, haiku, short stories, reviews and articles have appeared in magazines and journals in 37 countries.

Philip Knox (SHOp #21, 2006) no information available.

Chuck Kruger (SHOp #11, 2003) grew up in upstate New York. He and his wife Nell founded the Cape Clear Storytelling Festival. He has since retired to Pennsylvania.

Michael Laskey (SHOp #24, 2007) is a full time freelance poet, editor and tutor with many years' experience of promoting contemporary poetry. He lives in Suffolk in the UK.

Gerard Lee (SHOp #37, 2011) is a writer, actor and director who graduated with an M.Phil in Creative Writing from the Oscar Wilde Centre at Trinity College Dublin in 2007.

Michael Longley (SHOp #16, 2004), born in Belfast, was Ireland Professor of Poetry from 2007-10. Over 50 years he has spent time in County Mayo, which has inspired much of his poetry.

Eamonn Lynskey (SHOp #10, 2002) was nominated for Hennessy New Irish Writing Award and was a finalist in the Strokestown International Poetry Competition.

Peter Mabey (SHOp #9, 2002) is an architect, painter and sculptor. His work is on view in many galleries in West Cork.

John McAuliffe (SHOp #3, 2000) grew up in Listowel and has published five poetry collections. He co-directs the University of Manchester's Centre for New Writing.

Conor McCarthy (SHOp #8, 2002) is the author of four books, including *Seamus Heaney and Medieval Poetry*. He is Director of Philanthropy at the National Library of Australia.

Michael McCarthy (SHOp #18, 2005) grew up on a farm in West Cork. His first poetry collection *Birds' Nests and Other Poems* won the Patrick Kavanagh Award. Fr Michael died in 2018.

Ted McCarthy (SHOp #42, 2013) is a poet and translator living in Clones, County Monaghan. His work has appeared in magazines in Ireland, the UK, Germany, the USA, Canada and Australia.

Thomas McCarthy (SHOp #25, 2007) is an Irish poet, novelist, and critic. He attended University College Cork where he was part of a resurgence of literary activity under John Montague.

Padraic MacCana (SHOp #22, 2006) no information available

Clare McCotter (SHOp #43, 2013) lives in Derry. She won The British Haiku Award 2017 and The British Tanka Award 2013.

Dan McFadden (SHOp #30, 2009) no information available.

Afric McGlinchey (SHOp #34, 2010) has been a poet, journalist and freelance editor in Zimbabwe, South Africa and Ireland. Her auto-fictional prose poetry memoir comes out in 2021.

John McGrail (SHOp #20, 2006) no information available.

Niall McGrath (SHOp #32, 2010) is from Antrim, and has published five poetry collections and a novel.

Mary Turley McGrath (SHOp #43, 2013) is a poet and workshop facilitator. She has an M.Phil in Creative Writing from TCD, and is the author of four collections.

Medbh McGuckian (SHOp #40, 2012) studied with Seamus Heaney at Queen's University, and later returned as their first female writer-in-residence. She is the author of over 20 poetry collections.

Janis Mackay (SHOp #23, 2007) no information available.

John McKeown (SHOp #25, 2007) is a freelance arts journalist, a former theatre critic for the *Irish Daily Mail* and *Irish Independent*.

Brian Mackey (SHOp #2, 2000) no information available.

Michael McKimm (SHOp #36, 2011) lives in London. His publications include *Still This Need* (2009) and *Fossil Sunshine* (2013).

Michael Mackmin (SHOp #22, 2006) is a psychotherapist, poet and has been editor of *The Rialto* poetry magazine since it was established in 1985.

Brendan McMahon (SHOp #24, 2007) no information available.

Denise McSheehy (SHOp #45, 2014) lives in Devon. Her second collection *The Plate Spinner* was published in 2017.

Liz McSkeane (SHOp #6, 2001) is a poet and short story writer. She was born in Scotland to an Irish/Scottish family and has been living in Dublin since 1981.

Paul Maddern (SHOp #15, 2004) was born in Bermuda and moved to County Down in 2000. He is a Creative Writing Tutor for the Seamus Heaney Centre at Queen's University, Belfast.

Derek Mahon (SHOp #30, 2009) was born in Belfast and is widely regarded as one of the most talented and innovative Irish poets of the late 20th century. He won the Poetry Now Award in 2006 and 2009. He died in 2020.

Maitreyabandhu (SHOp #39, 2012) was born Ian Johnson in 1961, in Henley-in-Arden, Warwickshire. His first full-length poetry collection, *The Crumb Road*, was published in 2013.

Alwyn Marriage (SHOp #24, 2007) is a poet, lecturer, writer and Managing Editor of the publishing house Oversteps Books.

Shane Martin (SHOp #9, 2002) is a native of Carrickmacross in County Monaghan, now living in County Sligo. His third collection of poems is called *Thin Lines*.

Michael Massey (SHOp #15, 2004) was a poet and teacher from Kilkenny who died in 2014.

Paula Meehan (SHOp #46, 2014) has seven collections of poetry, most recently *Geomantic*. A former Ireland Professor of Poetry, she published *Imaginary Bonnets with Real Bees in Them* in 2016.

Valeria Melchioretto (SHOp #24, 2007) is Italian and was born in the German part of Switzerland. She moved to the UK in the 1990s and holds a degree in Modern Drama and an MA in Fine Art.

C.M. Millen (SHOp #43, 2013) won the 2011 Lee Bennett Hopkins Poetry Award for the best book of children's poetry published in the US for *The Ink Garden of Brother Theophane*.

Kate Miller (SHOp #28, 2008) won the Edwin Morgan International Poetry Prize in 2008. Her book *The Observances* (2015) won the Seamus Heaney Centre Prize for First Collection.

Geraldine Mills (SHOp #23, 2007) has several collections of short stories and poetry. She won the Hennessy/Tribune New Irish Writer Award and a Patrick and Katherine Kavanagh Fellowship.

Deborah Moffatt (SHOp #13, 2003) was born and raised in Vermont and has lived in Scotland since 1982. She writes poetry in both English and Gàidhlig, and has won prizes in both languages.

John Mole (SHOp #41, 2013) is an award-winning poet for adults and children, ex-teacher and jazz clarinettist.

Noel Monahan (SHOp #38, 2012) was born in Granard, County Longford and is the author of eight collections of poetry.

John Montague (SHOp #13, 2003) was born in New York and brought up in County Tyrone. He became the first Ireland Professor of Poetry in 1998. He died in 2016.

Fiona Moore (SHOp #33, 2010) lives in Greenwich. Her poems have appeared in various magazines including *The Poetry Review* and *Poetry London*.

Margaret Moore (SHOp #4, 2000) no information available.

Patrick Moran (SHOp #30, 2009) works as a post-primary teacher in County Tipperary. He has won the Gerard Manley Hopkins Poetry Prize and the 2008 Éist Poetry Competition.

Sinéad Morrissey (SHOp #5, 2001) was born in Portadown, County Armgah. She won the TS Eliot Prize in 2014 and the Forward Prize for Poetry in 2017.

Louis Mulcahy (SHOp #44, 2014) is a Dingle-based potter who writes poetry and short stories.

Paul Muldoon (SHOp #1, 1999) was born in County Armagh and has won a Pulitzer Prize for Poetry and the T. S. Eliot Prize. He held the post of Oxford Professor of Poetry from 1999 to 2004 and is Howard G.B. Clark '21 University Professor in the Humanities at Princeton University.

Gerry Murphy (SHOp #26, 2008) was born in Cork in 1952. His latest collection is *The Humours of Nothingness* (2020).

Helena Nelson (SHOp #17, 2005) is a poet, critic, publisher and the founding editor of *HappenStance Press*. She has lived in Fife, Scotland since 1977.

Eibhlin Nic Eochaidh (SHOp #29, 2009) is a Leitrim-based poet who won the 1999 Patrick Kavanagh Poetry Award.

Eiléan Ní Chuilleanáin (SHOp #38, 2012) is a poet, translator, and editor. She was appointed Ireland Professor of Poetry in 2016. Her *Collected Poems* will be published this autumn.

Doireann Ní Ghríofa (SHOp #46, 2014) lives in County Cork. She writes in both Irish and English and in 2016 won the Rooney Prize for Irish Literature.

Mary Noonan (SHOp #22, 2006) was born in London, but grew up in Cork. She lectures in French literature at University College Cork.

Robert Nye FRSL (SHOp #30, 2009) was an English poet and author. His bestselling novel *Falstaff* won both The Hawthornden Prize and Guardian Fiction Prize. He died in Cork in 2016.

Ruth O'Callaghan (SHOp #40, 2012) is a poet, mentor, critic, reviewer, adjudicator and workshop leader. Her work has been translated into numerous languages.

Eugene O'Connell (SHOp #46, 2014) has taught in St. Patrick's Boys School in Cork City for years. He has published two books of poetry and is a founding editor of the *Cork Literary Review.*

Anne O'Connor (SHOp #31, 2009) lives in Kilkenny. She has had poems published in the *Kilkenny Poetry Broadsheet, Cyphers, Poetry Ireland Review, Revival Press* and other publications.

Karen O'Connor (SHOp #43, 2013) has won the Listowel Writers' Week Single Poem Prize, The Allingham Poetry Award, and The Jonathan Swift Creative Writing Award for Poetry.

Michael O'Dea (SHOp #34, 2010) was born in County Roscommon and short-listed for the Hennessy/Sunday Tribune awards and placed third in the Patrick Kavanagh Poetry Competition.

Bernard O'Donoghue (SHOp #27, 2008) lives in Oxford. He was shortlisted for the T.S. Eliot Prize and succeeded Seamus Heaney as Honorary President of the Irish Literary Society of London.

Gregory O'Donoghue (SHOp #20, 2006) published his first book when he was 24 and became the youngest poet to be included in the *Faber Book of Irish Verse*. He died in 2005.

Peadar O'Donoghue (SHOp #44, 2014) is a poet, photographer and co-editor at PB Press.

Ita O'Donovan (SHOp #13, 2003) was born in Cork and now lives in Clifden. In 2017 her poetry was shortlisted for two editions of *The Irish Times*, Hennessy New Irish Writing.

Gréagóir Ó Dúill (SHOp #13, 2003) was born in Dublin in 1946. He has worked as a lecturer of contemporary Irish-language poetry in Queen's University, Belfast and in the University of Ulster.

Desmond O'Grady (SHOp #8, 2002) was a poet, translator and writer. He had a PhD in Celtic languages from Harvard and later taught in universities in Egypt and Rome. He died in 2014.

John O'Leary (SHOp #3, 2000) was an award-winning poet, breeder of Irish draught horses and sheep farmer who drowned in 2012 in a sailing accident off the West Cork coast.

Mary O'Malley (SHOp #5, 2001) was on the Committee of the Cúirt International Poetry Festival for eight years. She was the Trinity Writer Fellow at the Oscar Wilde Centre for 2019.

Liam Ó Muirthile (SHOp #4, 2000) was a prominent Irish-language poet and journalist who also wrote plays and novels. He was a member of a group of poets from UCC who collaborated in the late 1960s in the journal *Innti*, the format of which The SHOp was based. He died in 2018.

Paul O'Prey (SHOp #40, 2012) no information available.

Ciarán O'Rourke (SHOp #31, 2009) is based in Dublin and was the winner of the Lena Maguire/ Cúirt New Irish Writing Award 2009, the Westport Poetry Prize 2015 and the Fish Poetry Prize 2016.

Cathal Ó Searcaigh (SHOp #9, 2002) was born in County Donegal and is a modern Irish language poet. His work includes poetry, plays and travelogues.

Leanne O'Sullivan (SHOp #23, 2007) won the Lawrence O'Shaughnessy Award for Irish Poetry in 2011. In 2010 she was awarded the Rooney Prize for Irish Literature.

Michelle O'Sullivan (SHOp #39, 2012) was born in Chicago and grew up in County Sligo. Her first collection, *The Blue End of Stars*, was shortlisted for the Michael Murphy Memorial Prize.

Alice Oswald (SHOp #6, 2001) is the author of eight books of poetry. Elected as the University of Oxford Professor of Poetry in 2019, she lives in Bristol in the UK.

Susan O'Toole (SHOp #10, 2002) is known for her Ballydehob Mermaid. One of her sculptures was shown at the '15e Biennale de Lausanne.' She continues to sculpt and write.

Seán Ó Tuama (SHOp #25, 2007) was an Irish poet, playwright and academic. He was the Professor of Irish Literature at University College Cork and a visiting professor at Harvard, Oxford and Toronto universities. He died in 2006.

David Page (SHOp #30, 2009) is a painter and writer based in Tobermory, Isle of Mull, and Kells, Northern Ireland.

William Palmer (SHOp #17, 2005) is a poet and novelist. His study of writers and drink, *In Love with Hell*, will be published in 2021.

Gwyn Parry (SHOp #27, 2008) lived on Anglesey for much of his life before becoming a graphic designer in Cardiff and Aberystwyth. He now lives and works in Dublin.

Jo Pestel (SHOp #5, 2001) no information available.

Colin Pink (SHOp #46 2014) is an art historian and poet based in London.

Andrea Porter (SHOp #26, 2008) lives in the Fens near Cambridge. She has been published in a number of poetry and online magazines in the UK, USA and Australia.

Peter Porter (SHOp #7, 2001) was a British-based Australian poet. In 2007, he was made a Royal Society of Literature Companion of Literature. He died in 2010.

Edward Power (SHOp #12, 2003) was a Kilkenny-based poet who died at the age of 68 in 2019.

John Prior (SHOp #38, 2012) no information available.

Philip Quirke (SHOp #36, 2012) is an author, teacher and poet based in Wexford.

Billy Ramsell (SHOp #14, 2004) is a poet and educational publisher based in Cork. In 2013 he was awarded the Ireland Chair of Poetry Bursary. His first published poem appeared in The SHOp.

Peter Redgrove (SHOp #6, 2001) was a British poet who also wrote prose, novels and plays with his second wife, Penelope Shuttle. He died in 2003.

Frank Redpath (SHOp #1, 1999) was one of the ten poets in Douglas Dunn's 1982 anthology of Hull poets, *A Rumoured City*. He died in 1990.

Daphne Rock (SHOp #17, 2007) was a poet, teacher, amateur geologist and grandmother of eight. She died in 2008.

Padraig Rooney (SHOp #35, 2011) studied at Maynooth College and at the Sorbonne. He won the Strokestown International Poetry Prize in 2009. He lives in Basel, Switzerland.

Mark Roper (SHOp #4, 2000) was brought up in North London. In 1980 he moved to County Kilkenny where he has lived ever since. He was Editor of *Poetry Ireland* for 1999.

Sue Rose (SHOp #30, 2009) is a poet and literary translator and has published novels in translation by authors such as Florian Zeller, Nicolas Fargues and Olivier Adam.

Gabriel Rosenstock (SHOp #39, 2012) is a poet, tankaist, haikuist, novelist, essayist, playwright, blogger and translator who works chiefly in the Irish language.

Carol Rumens (SHOp #1, 1999) has written poetry, plays, non-fiction, translations and a novel. She was Poetry Editor of *Quarto* and the *Literary Review* in the 1980s.

Denise Ryan (SHOp #39, 2012) is a writer of contemporary poetry from Dublin. In 2010, Denise was selected to write a series of poems for the National Famine Commemoration.

Mo Ryan (SHOp #33, 2010) no information available.

Peter Salisbury (SHOp #32, 2010) grew up in Chester and is a filmmaker and writer who runs drama and screenwriting workshops.

Peter Sansom (SHOp #21, 2006) is a poet and tutor who has led writing workshops in schools and workplaces for over 25 years. He is a director of The Poetry Business in Huddersfield.

Clare Sawtell (SHOp #44, 2014) lives near Kinvara in County Galway. She is a cellist and teaches at Coole Music in Gort. Her most recent poetry collection is *The Next Dance*.

Eileen Sheehan (SHOp #2, 2000) lives in Killarney. Her third collection, *The Narrow Way of Souls,* was launched in May 2018.

Donald Sheehy (SHOp #28, 2008) no information available.

Rhiannon Shelley (SHOp #17, 2005) was at one time the assistant editor of The SHOp. Daughter of John and Hilary Wakeman, she died in 2019.

Stephen Shields (SHOp #37, 2011) lives in Athenry, County Galway. His work has been published widely in Ireland and the UK in *West 47/ Cuirt Annual, Crannog, Envoi* and *Equinox* among others.

George Shorten (SHOp #20, 2006) no information available.

Penelope Shuttle (SHOp #2, 2000) has lived in Cornwall since 1970 and is the widow of the poet Peter Redgrove. *Redgrove's Wife* was shortlisted for the Forward Prize and T.S. Eliot Prize in 2006.

Annette Skade (SHOp #38, 2012) is a poet and teacher living on the Beara peninsula. In July 2013 she launched her inaugural poetry collection, *Thimblerig,* at the West Cork Literary Festival.

K.V. Skene (SHOp #25, 2007) is a Canadian poet whose poetry has been published internationally in Canadian US, UK, Australia, Austria, Ireland and Indian journals and anthologies.

Knute Skinner (SHOp #10, 2002) has lived in Killaspuglonane, County Clare for the past 55 years. He is the author of sixteen books of verse including *Fifty Years: Poems 1957-2007.*

Floyd Skloot (SHOp #10, 2002) is a poet, novelist and science writer. Born in Brooklyn and now living in Portland, Oregon, he is the author of numerous books of poetry, fiction and nonfiction.

Joan Jobe Smith (SHOp #8, 2002) is a founding editor of *Pearl* and *Bukowski Review*. For a decade she enjoyed/endured a literary and platonic friendship with the writer Charles Bukowski.

Gerard Smyth (SHOp #41, 2013) is now retired from a lifetime's work as a journalist with *The Irish Times*, but continues as its poetry editor. His tenth collection is out this year.

Cherry Smyth (SHOp #32, 2010) is a poet, novelist and critic based in London. She teaches poetry at the University of Greenwich and was a Royal Literary Fellow, 2014-2016.

Gillian Somerville-Large is a writer and the wife of Peter Somerville-Large.

Breda Spaight (SHOp #44, 2014) has appeared in *The Honest Ulsterman, Poetry Ireland Review, The Singing Fly* (featured poet), *The Interpreter's House* (featured poet) and elsewhere.

Dolores Stewart (SHOp #14, 2004) is a bliningual poet from the West of Ireland. Her first collection, *In Out of the Rain*, was published in 1999 and *Presence of Mind* in 2005.

Paul Stubbs (SHOp #44, 2014) is the author of six poetry collections and of two books of poetical and philosophical essays. His latest collection is *The Lost Songs of Gravity* (2020).

George Szirtes is a Hungarian-born poet and translator.

Betty Thompson (SHOp #26, 2008) is a poet and author of 'Elegy for Donal McCann'.

Frances Thompson (SHOp #3, 2000) was born in Belfast in 1944. She taught in Northern Ireland, North Africa and London, before settling in Devon, where she still lives.

Anthony Thwaite (SHOp #41, 2013) is an English poet and critic, now widely known as the editor of his friend Philip Larkin's collected poems and letters.

Richard Toovey (SHOp #32, 2010) no information available.

David Trame (SHOp #24, 2007) is an Italian teacher of English, born and living in Venice. He has been published in around 200 literary magazines in the UK, US and elsewhere.

Deborah Tyler-Bennett (SHOp #18, 2005) has published eight volumes of poems and three volumes of short linked stories. She is working on her first novel, *Livin' in a Great Big Way*.

Peter Van Belle (SHOp #29, 2009) lives and works in Belgium. He has published poetry and short stories in the US, Ireland, New Zealand, Canada, Belgium and the UK.

Fred Voss (SHOp #5, 2001) is an American poet and novelist who has written about the lives of American machinists working in factories for over 40 years.

Jenny Vuglar (SHOp #35, 2011) was born in New Zealand but has lived in London since l979. She has had poems and stories published in various magazines and anthologies.

John Wakeman (SHOp #46, 2014) was the editor of two 2-volume works, *World Authors* and *World Film Directors* (HW Wilson County, NY), and the founder and editor of The SHOp.

William Wall (SHOp #46, 2014) was the 2017 winner of the Drue Heinz Prize for Literature and has also won Virginia Faulkner Award, The Sean O'Faoláin Prize, and The Patrick Kavanagh Award. He was longlisted for the Man Booker Prize and The Manchester Fiction Prize.

Niall R. Walsh (SHOp #26, 2008) no information available.

Tony Weston (SHOp #46, 2014) was a poet, potter, artist, instrument maker, and builder. His daily front-window poems were enjoyed by neighbours in Bridport, Dorset. He died in 2020.

David Wheatley (SHOp #1, 1999) is an Irish poet and critic. He studied at Trinity College Dublin where he edited *Icarus*. He is the author of four volumes of poetry and lives in rural Aberdeenshire.

Adam White (SHOp #46, 2014) studied English and French at NUI Galway, where he began reading and writing poetry. He lives in the west of France.

Ian Wild (SHOp #21, 2006) is a writer, composer and theatre worker from Enniskean, County Cork. In 2009 he won the Fish International Short Story Prize.

Saint James Harris Wood (SHOp #46, 2014) was released from a California penal colony in 2019 after serving 20 years. He has reinvented himself as a poet and writer of the darkly absurd.

Macdara Woods (SHOp #4, 2000) was married to the current Ireland Professor of Poetry, Eiléan Ni Chuilleanáin, with whom he was co-founder and editor of the journal *Cyphers*. He died in 2018.

Anna Woodford (SHOp #25, 2007) is a poet based in Newcastle. Her poetry collection *Birdhouse* won the Crashaw Prize and was included in the Guardian's round up of best poetry books of the year.

Mary Woodward (SHOp #28, 2008) was born in Hammersmith to Irish and Welsh parents. She has a Master's degree for research on William Morris's early poetry from the University of Liverpool.

Abigail A. Zammit (SHOp #39, 2012) is from the island of Malta. She holds a PhD in Creative Writing (Lancaster) and has had poems published in various British and Canadian journals.

Artists and Photographers

Nick Bridson Baker is an ex-cartoonist, now doing monotype prints and paintings in his shed. His poems have been published in a number of magazines.

Beverley Gene Coraldean is an illustrator and screen printer working in Norwich. Her business name is Genealityart.

Luis Fanti no information available.

Valerie Gleeson no information available.

Denise Hogan is a graduate of GMIT in print and paint, specialising in monoprints, aquatints and paintings. She has exhibited extensively and has works in many private and corporate collections.

Alice Hoult is a multidisciplinary artist with a background in theatre and performance. See www.alicemalia.net.

Hammond Journeaux was born in New Zealand and lives in West Cork. She was the cover artist of the second issue of The SHOp.

Brian Lalor is a printmaker and writer, and currently curator of the Ballydehob Arts Museum. The image on the cover of this anthology is a woodcut from a sequence illustrating Samuel Taylor Coleridge's *The Rime of the Ancient Mariner*.

Mary Norman was a printmaker and illustrator. She and her husband John Mole produced the Signal Award-winning book of poems for children *Boo to a Goose*. She died in 2016.

Jeanette McCulloch says 'Collaborating with other creatives and especially poets opens up possibilities for me to respond each time afresh. That is the joy of being an artist.'

John Minihan is a photographer best known for his early pictures of the ordinary people of Athy, and later for his photographs of writers and poets, especially of Samuel Beckett.

Peadar O'Donoghue is a poet, photographer, and co-editor at PB Press.

Joakim Säflund is an artist working primarily but not exclusively with painting. Born in 1963 he is currently living and working in Sydney.

Edwin Smith was an English photographer best known for his distinctive vignettes of English gardens, landscapes and architecture. He died in 1971.

Matt Wakeman is an artist-gardener, living in Norwich, UK.

Theo Wakeman is an artist who lived in West Cork for many years, and is now in Norfolk, UK.